TRUTH ENCOUNTERS

BY FELICIA MURRELL

Endorsements for Truth Encounters

Growing up learning to read early in life has caused me to develop a love for good books. "Truth Encounters" penned by Felicia Murrell would be categorized by me as a real life action thriller that the reader can identify with. It grabs your attention from the very beginning with her life experiences, yet the one ingredient that Felicia adds that most books of this kind leave out is the application process of overcoming these very same scenarios in the readers' own life. I can relate to her mess, that she is very transparent about sharing, but that she turned into a message of overcoming. All to often people live as victims when you encounter life situations like the ones Felicia shares. I was engaged throughout the whole book. Its one of those books that you have to force yourself to put down. It offers hope to become what you were intended to be in life all along. Get this one if you are serious about getting unstuck in life's situational circumstances.

Trisha Frost
Co-Founder/President of Shiloh Place Ministries
Author: *Unbound: Breaking Free of Life's Entanglements*

Truth Encounters is a beautifully redemptive book in which the Father Heart of God is the hero in the story. My dear friend Felicia is a living breathing example of how the power of God's love can completely transform a life. I promise if you embark on this journey with her, your life will be forever changed.

Sherri L. Lewis, MD
Founder of Bethel Cameroon School of Supernatural Ministry,
Missionary, Essence Magazine Best Selling Author: *My Soul Cries Out,*
Selling My Soul, Dance Into Destiny, Finding Mrs. Wright, Becoming
Mrs. Right, The List and Bessem's Song

This book is dedicated to my brother John...my rescue hero. I love you with all my heart. Thank you for being the best big brother a little girl could ever have. You were my lifeline. May you encounter Truth in every part of you.

TABLE OF CONTENTS

PROLOGUE

When I was sixteen I committed a legal crime. I would have gotten away scot clean if it hadn't been for that boy's mama calling mine. I'd like to say I wasn't in my right mind. I'd like to say someone held a gun to my head and forced my decision. I'd like to say it wasn't my fault. To say any of those things would simply be for the sole purpose of gaining sympathy with you and making myself feel better about my actions.

The truth is, I was very much aware of my choice; even though I conveniently blamed it all on my boyfriend at the time. The truth is, I sold my today in exchange for a happier version of tomorrow. The truth is, I am responsible for every duplicit decision leading up to and after I committed my crime.

Looking back, I can't say I would have done things differently. Although, I convinced myself that I would. I even set about to recreate the wrong so I could have the opportunity to do it right the second time. Oh the tricks the mind plays when one is writhe with guilt and shame.

At the time, it seemed like the right thing to do, the only thing to do. I was out of options. It was kill or be killed. And that's exactly what would have happened to me if my momma found out I was pregnant.

I couldn't believe I waited this long. I should've had a clue after missing one or two cycles. I tried the clothes hanger trick for weeks but that didn't work. I punched myself in the stomach, tried everything I knew to get the blood flowing. Going into month four of no cycle, I knew I needed to get a test. The trick was trying to buy a pregnancy test in a small town at a store where somebody didn't know me, Bo, my momma, his mama... Trouble with living in a small town, the world always talkin' 'bout six degrees of separation, hmph, in a small town, it's more like three degrees of separation cause e'erbody know somebody who know somebody. As luck would have it, I managed to find a local drug store where a white girl was working so that was good. White people and black people in our town didn't mix much. Other than being in classes and band together, playing sports together or maybe working an after school job together, we were all one generation away from white sheets so we just kept to ourselves. I'd barely peed on the stick good before the little plus sign appeared. Damn! What had I gone and done now? I was up a creek without a paddle. If I thought this fool loved me, the truth sho'll came to light when I told him I was pregnant.

Bo was po' and didn't want a baby anyway. He was headed to college on a baseball scholarship and didn't want anything to ruin his chances of doing better for himself than his momma or daddy had done for him. I could've ran away, but where to? Girls' homes didn't really exist any more. That was only something I'd read about in books from the library. I blamed Bo and said it was all his fault. When I told him, he acted like I was trying to trap him. Truth be told, I ain't want to have no baby by a dumb ass jock. I ain't want to have no baby period. After watching my momma and daddy's loveless marriage, I ain't want no parts of the family way.

Still in denial, I called my pediatrician's office and made an appointment. I'm not sure what I was hoping for in going to see the doctor. I guess I was hoping the stick test was wrong. I knew what they were going to say. I guess I was really hoping they would give me the contact info for a legit clinic. Even though I'd tried the clothes hanger on myself, I didn't need to be found dead in some back alley because of a botched procedure. To my surprise, not only did they give me contact info, they made the appointment for me. Doc told me I had to go quick cause I was already twenty weeks and they wouldn't do a "procedure" after twenty-two weeks gestation. Whatever that meant. I was sixteen. I had no clue. All I was thinking about was the $400 I'd get to pocket 'cause Doc also said my daddy's insurance would pay for the "procedure". That was a relief. I'd already told Bo if he wanted me to kill the baby, he was gonna have to pay for it. I didn't feel I should tell him any different. I felt like I deserved that money. After all, I had convinced myself that he made me do it.

Truth was, I didn't want no baby at sixteen. I was smart. I hated small town life. My smarts was my ticket out. I knew if I kept up my grades and tested well on all those big tests, somebody somewhere would pay my way through college. I was black. I was a female and a first generation college attendee to boot. Well not really, but a small lie never hurt nothing. I had already made up my mind. In two years, I was packing up my little brown Chevrolet Nova and leaving small town life behind. Good riddance to Bo with no aspirations and no goals. Sayonara to my parents whom I could never seem to please. Hasta la vista to shallow friends, fake people, racist living and small town limitations. Living in the country stifled my dreams. If I had a baby, everybody would expect me to stay and go to the county technical college. That was a death sentence to my escape plan. I wasn't having that. So it really did come down to kill or be killed. But, if it was really that simple, why did I shed silent tears all the way to the clinic?

That morning, I rode the bus to school like nothing doing. Met up with Fran in the school parking lot and left in her car headed to the big city. I stared out the window looking at nothing in particular and cried the whole way. I must have had a hard time breathing through my nose from all the tears. Fran looked over and said, "You know, you don't have to do this. We can turn around and go back." With no courage to find my voice, I simply shook my head no and kept staring out the window. My head shook from side to side, but inside I had just had a whole dialogue, "I can't. Bo will kill me. My mom will kill me. My dad will be so hurt. I know y'all like this small town, but this is not me. I can't get stuck here. I'm the good girl, the smart girl. I take AP classes. My mom's a preacher. What would my teachers think? What would my pastor say? My Grams would be so disappointed..." and so the conversation went. And the tears kept falling.

   As we neared the clinic, a different kind of fear overtook me. What if there were picketers out there? What if there was a news crew there? Part of me hoped for a picketer who might suggest taking me away until I could have the baby and give it up for adoption. The other part of me was just plain scared to death.

   I don't know what I expected, a big sign that said "Abortions here" with a neon arrow pointing down but it wasn't like that at all. We drove to this quiet, dismal street and almost missed the building cause there was no sign at all. Just a two story, clapboard structure that reminded me of old, distressed wood when it's been wet but starting to dry – half dark, half faded. On the side of the door was a small, nondescript white 5x7 sign that read in black letters: Family Planning Clinic. I couldn't help but laugh at the irony. Inside, the dismal feeling didn't let up. The clinic was quiet, every face grim. The carpet was tannish yellow and threadbare. The chairs were plastic and hard. The fluorescent light bulb was noticeably dim and hummed a woeful tune. The lady behind the counter told the saddest tale with the jaunt set of her eyes and the firm set of her mouth. This place felt like a funeral home. No laughter. No music, hardly any movement. No noise, just the hum of the light bulb. When the bell jingled over the door to announce a new entry, people looked up and then quickly away.

   I signed in and took a seat in one of those cold, hard black plastic chairs. Wringing my hands, I looked for something to read to distract me from my racing thoughts. Noticeably absent were magazines with bright colors, anything that depicted life, fun, vitality, or health. I did, however, become a scholar on STD's, herpes, and vaginal warts. Blue pamphlets on syphilis and gonorrhea lay on every table. Green pamphlets with information on herpes and vaginal warts were their companions. I was embarrassed when the lady called my name and looked at the green pamphlet in my hand then back at me.

   Sheepishly, I sat the thing down on my seat and followed her through the door. She introduced herself and pointed to another cold, hard black plastic chair instructing me to take a seat. This room had no overhead light whatsoever. Daylight crept in through the closed blinds to cast a shadow in the room. The door was left ajar so the light from the hallway filtered into the room. A small desk lamp was lit to illuminate the clipboard she held in her hand.

She sat down in her high back, top grain, brown leather executive desk chair placing the clipboard on her desk looked directly at me and asked, "Why are you here?" I must have looked dumbstruck because she asked the question again, this time staring at the clipboard instead of looking into the eyes of my soul. Inside my head, my voice answered, "To kill my baby," but out of my mouth, I hung my head and said, "I'm pregnant." Next, she asked in a stern voice, "Well, have you considered other options?" Again my head, in a smart alek voice, shouted at her, "Would I be killing my baby if I had other options? Are you stupid?" But out of my mouth came, "I don't have any." And so it went back and forth, "What did your mom say?" "My mom doesn't know." "What about the guy? His family?" "The guy don't care. His family gave him the money to give to me to kill the baby." "Have you ever had a termination before?" Me: "No". Her: "It's not painful. They will use a vacuum like tube to suction out the fetal tissue from the lining of your uterus. You won't feel any pain and in a few minutes it will all be over."

On and on she talked. And all the while, my heart was talking to my head, "A few minutes to make a baby. A few minutes to kill it. I couldn't believe I was doing this. I'm a Christian. My Big Grandma would die if she knew what I was doing. My momma would kill me if she found out I was pregnant. I don't want to be stuck in no small town. I don't have a choice. I've got to go through with this. I'm killing my baby. I can't believe I'm doing this."

My thoughts were interrupted. "Did you hear me?" "Uh?" I said, giving the lady a blank stare. "I'm gonna get the nurse. Are you gonna be okay? You sure you want to do this? You've thought this through?" I looked at her in the eye and nodded my head up and down as she left the room. I willed myself not to cry. I was grown enough to get myself into this mess. I had to be grown enough to get myself out of it. SIXTEEN! I'm sixteen for crying out loud! I wanted my momma. No, I couldn't. She would kill me. It's kill or be killed.

"Okay, you can follow me." I think the lady was relieved to be handing me off. Someone else introduced herself to me. She had a much nicer disposition than the lady behind the front counter and the lady in that dark room. She said they were going to see how far along I was. I laid down on the table for something called an ultrasound. She put this cold gel stuff on my belly and I began to hear a sound, "Whoosh. Whoosh." And then, "Thump, thump, thump, thump, thump." When I turned my head towards the noise, she turned the sound all the way down so I couldn't hear it. I turned my head back towards the wall. Every room was dark, barely lit. Trying to take my mind off the sound, I wondered if that was intentional. I turned again to see what was going on. I looked at the TV screen and there in black and white was the form of a little ball, kind of like a kitten all curled up. I couldn't take my eyes off the screen. That was my baby. There on the screen was the baby I was getting ready to kill. 'Oh my gosh. Oh my gosh. What am I doing?'

Perhaps my breathing intensified. Perhaps I sighed or said aloud what my heart was screaming. I don't know. But the lady turned to see me watching that TV screen and shifted her body so that all I could see was her backside in those fuchsia pink scrubs. I got the message loud and clear that I wasn't suppose to be looking so I turned my head back to the wall with no pictures and stared at the wooden planks with the little pine knots in them that formed the wall.

After she was finished, she turned to me and said they would need to do a D&E and asked had I ever heard of that before. Overwhelmed still by the sight and sound of what I'd just experienced, I didn't trust my voice to refrain from the tears that were flowing in my heart so I shook my head no. She went on to say because of how far along I was they would need to insert laminaria, which is something like seaweed, into my cervix to open it up. So they would do that and then have me come back in about two and half hours. She left the room to give me some privacy while I undressed and slipped on that piece of paper they have in the doctor's office to cover you up. A minute or two later, she knocked and reentered the room. She had me slide down on the table and place my feet in stirrups. I was familiar with these. I became sexually active the summer before my thirteenth birthday so every time

I went to see Doc, she used these to check me out down below. The nurse inserted the speculum and began to widen it or whatever it is they do down there. "You'll feel a pinch," I heard her say. Back to the wooden wall I stared. That over, she softly said, "you can get dressed now. Be sure to come back, okay?"

It took everything in me to do just that. Silently, I walked down the narrow corridor back through the door I entered, over what seemed like an eternity ago. I looked for my friend, Fran, and found her reading the same green pamphlet I had discarded. Our eyes locked. With a grimace, she sat down the pamphlet and stood. We headed for the door. "Are you okay?" she asked. I nodded my head yes wishing for a place where I could go and cry my eyes out. Wishing for someone in my life who loved me enough to promise me this would all be okay. Wishing I could go back and make a different choice. Wishing I could go home and not return in two and a half hours. "Where to now?" she asked.

I explained all that was said and suggested we go eat. We found a Pizza Hut and ordered pizza with some of the money Bo's family had given him to give to me to kill my baby. I barely touched my food. Fran looked at her watch. We still had over an hour and a half to wait. I couldn't go back there and wait. It was too depressing. I suggested we go to the mall. Desperately grasping at something, anything that would take my mind off the seaweed now embedded inside my cervix to help me kill my baby.

At the mall, I found myself in the local Christian bookstore. I felt like such a hypocrite. I didn't even know why I was in there. I was just drawn to the store. I looked at everything. I looked at nothing. Maybe I was secretly hoping for a Christian with a sixth sense that would just "know" I was pregnant and whisk me away to safety. Wasn't there anyone who would save me from myself? Where was the person who would save my baby? Had it really come down to kill or be killed? The war raged within me. We walked the mall. I remembered nothing. All I could think about was escaping this hellish nightmare. I didn't want to commit suicide. I had too much going for myself to die. But, I really wanted to run away. Maybe I should have just asked Fran to take me to the Greyhound bus station and disappear. Where would I go? I had no one. I had nowhere to turn. And what about this seaweed? What would happen if I didn't go back? Nah. At this point, I was committed to going through with it. I had to.

Finally, we headed back to the clinic. No picketers. No TV crews. No cars. Nothing. This street, this place, was as dead as my baby was about to be.

We parked in the same graveled lot. We walked down the same concrete steps. I stared at the same nondescript white sign with black letters. I opened the door. The bell jingled. The lady behind the counter looked up at me and then down. I signed in. Again. No one else was in the waiting area. I sat down again. I could not do the pamphlets again so I stared ahead at the beige wall and wondered how many other girls had come in and killed their babies while I was at the mall.

A minute passed and the door opened. The nurse looked at me. I got up to follow. Down the long corridor we went. I passed the first dark room on my left where I confessed to having no options. I passed the second dark room on my left where the whoosh sound and the thumping sound were still echoing from that machine. At least I could faintly hear it in my heart as I walked by. My destination this time was the room on the right. It was well lit. Surgically clean.

I was instructed to undress and put on another paper thing. A few minutes passed and finally, there was a knock at the door. A white male entered. He was 6'3", athletic build, gray hair, dressed in surgical garb: cap, scrubs, booties, mask. He offered a slight smile, like the doctor who is about to tell his patient bad news. The same nurse from the ultrasound room followed him into the room. Her fuchsia scrubs now covered with a hospital robe, cap on her head, booties, and a mask. They eyed each other. Both faces suddenly became grim. No one smiled. The doctor's voice was soft. His eyes were apologetic. He explained again what the counselor lady had already told me. He patted my shoulder and said this should only take a few minutes. I laid back on the table, as he instructed me to, slid down towards the bottom and placed my feet in another set of stirrups. Gently the doctor said, "I'm going to touch you." The sound of a machine hissing and humming filled the room.

I closed my eyes to the horror of what was happening around me. I heard a heavy sigh and opened my eyes with a start. The nurse looked at me and then at the doc. The doctor said, "I'm sorry. This is taking much longer than expected." I closed my eyes and in that moment all the will power I had mustered to keep the tears at bay was lost. I began to cry and my chest heaved and heaved. In that moment, my life was forever changed. Like the lady in the *Scarlet Letter* who was forced to walk around with the A embroidered on her clothing for everyone to see, I felt like a big K had been branded across my chest and my life would be forever marred by the fact that I had now become a baby killer. At sixteen, I had committed a legal crime for which there was no way for me to pay recompense for my evil deed. I was henceforth now and forever more, eternally damned.

I don't know when the doctor and nurse left. I think I remember her saying I could get dressed now. But there I lay, crying and crying. In complete and utter disbelief of what my life had become. How did I end up here? I'm the smart girl. I'm the good girl. Right? But the Big K across my chest told a completely different story. Obviously, I had been fooling myself and had done a good job of it. At some point, I managed to get up, get dressed and take the long walk down the corridor to the waiting area. I pushed open the door and my eyes locked with Fran. She got up and came towards me. I was so thankful for her hug. She pulled away and grabbed my arms. Looking into my eyes she asked, "Are you okay?" I shook my head yes, but my tear stained face told a different story. The lady at the counter busied herself with something on her desk as we walked out the door so she didn't have to look our way.

Past the nondescript sign, up the concrete steps, to the graveled parking lot, into the car, and down the highway back to our small town, we drove. Fran dropped me off at the local grocery store where I was a cashier. I retrieved my blue polyester grocery store vest from the book bag I had taken on the bus to convince myself and others that it was just a routine day in the life of a sixteen year old headed to school and then to work. I worked a five-hour shift. My mom picked me up from work. I went home, closed the door to my room and silently cried myself to sleep.

Up the next morning, I showered. Dressed in my royal blue sweatshirt with white italic lettering that read, "There is life in the blood" complete with the scripture reference Leviticus 17:11 stamped underneath the quote and feeling completely hypocritical, I went to school. A very normal day. Life returned to normal, or at least I thought it had.

Three days later, I was asleep on Bo's couch and when I woke up, my Big Boy Burger jacket that I had "forgotten" to return when I left the employ of the burger place was wet to the touch. I unzipped it thinking, "That's strange." The whole front of my shirt was soaked through. My shirt, my jacket, the couch, everything was wet and it smelled like spoiled milk. That's odd, I thought to myself. I borrowed a t-shirt from Bo's sister and headed home so I could shower and change. The next morning, same thing. I woke up, chest wet and my room smelled like spoiled milk. And then, it hit me like a ton of bricks! This was my baby's milk. Oh my gosh! My body knew there was no longer a baby in there so all of the milk was draining out. And I began to cry again. 'What have I done? WHAT HAVE I DONE? I'm a baby killer.'

I killed my baby. I've got to make this right. How do I make it right? And all I can think is that if I could do it over, I wouldn't make the same choice again. No matter what Bo said I would NOT kill my baby a second time. So, what do I do? I go back to sleeping with Bo so I can make it right. The only way I know to make it right was to go back and have the choice again and this time choose to keep my baby, no matter what it costs me. That sounded like a novel idea until the third time Bo and I were doing it. In the middle of it, I found myself praying to God, "God, please don't let me get pregnant."

I realized how stupid I was. Here I was with somebody that didn't love me, didn't even want to have a baby with me, was using me for sex and money, didn't care a thing about me and I was trying to fix a mistake with someone I didn't even want a life with. That's dumb. 'Nah,

I'm a just take this blood money and spend it and bide my time. And then when I graduate, I'm a leave this no count fool, this town, and all these bad memories right here.'

That would have worked too, but Bo's sister saw me shopping in a local department store and told his momma that I lied about being pregnant just to get money from their family. So now she done up and called my momma and asked her if I was really pregnant. And my momma didn't even know. Fortunately for me, by the time Bo's momma made the call, I had already had the abortion or my momma would have made me keep that baby. Hmm, was that really fortunate? There I go again all conflicted and confused about what I have done.

Momma hung up the phone and said, "That was Ms. Roslyn." I looked her in the face and nodded once. Momma continued," Ms. Roslyn said you are pregnant and Bo gave you money to have an abortion. She wanted to know if that was true. Is it true?" As I looked at her, anger welled up inside of me. The K brand on my chest was all aflame in guilt. "Yes, it's true," I said to her, "I was pregnant." "Was?" She asked. "Yes, I was." "So, you had an abortion?" "Yes," I replied. "When?" She asked. "About a month ago," I said. I was expecting her to say something more. Yell, scream, get mad, be sad, hug me, hit me, anything. She looked at me. Walked from the sink to the stove and began stirring the pot of food she was cooking. Left looking at her back, I sighed; walked out to my car and headed to work.

In the car, I cried. I cried big huge crocodile tears. I cried for the baby I killed. I cried for the little girl in me that longed to be loved by a momma who didn't know how. I cried for the boy I'd given myself to and worked to support, squandering the money I was saving for college to do things for his sorry tail behind. I cried because I was alone. I cried because I would have loved to make a different choice. I cried because I couldn't change what happened. I couldn't fix it. I couldn't make it better. I couldn't get the Big K off my chest. I was branded. I was eternally damned. No one could ever know. No one could ever hurt me that much again.

And there, in my little car, with my work vest soaked in as much tears as my baby's milk, I vowed to never let anyone close enough to hurt me that way again. Anger and rage became my friend. Mistrust and suspicion became my constant companions. I hated this town. I hated these people. I hated my parents. I hated Bo. But most of all, I hated myself.

Besides me, Bo, his family and Fran, only one other person knew that I'd been knocked up. One day, in a fit of stupid, I told my friend, Christina. Now all of a sudden, I was getting eyes and looks from everyone in the hallway. I didn't know if Chris opened her mouth and told somebody who told somebody or if Bo's little sister, Trina, let the cat out of the bag.

First bell, I had office and I was running an errand for Dr. Humboldt, our principal. On my way back, I heard someone calling me. I turned and approaching me was Harold Nichols, only the finest piece of short, stocky milk chocolate specimen to stand at five feet tall. He sidled over to me with a crooked grin and said, "So, is it true?" "Is what true?" I asked. "The rumor is Bo Carter done got you knocked up." I looked him in the face, not flinching, that dreaded K aflame on my chest. I said nothing. "It is," he said and smiled like a big old chess cat. "Is that a badge for me or a badge for him?" I asked, referring to the smile he was displaying like a badge of honor. Harold shrugged his shoulders and replied, "Guess I just never expected a girl like you to get knocked up."

He knew I was putting out. We'd already had a secret round in his Buick that no one knew about. OK, well, my friend, Alisa knew. Hard to keep a score like that to yourself. I continued to stare. The word was just leaking out that I was pregnant and now I have no baby. What was I going to do? Finally, I said to Harold, "I need to get back," and I walked away. Bypassing the office altogether, I swiftly walked into the nearest bathroom, did a quick feet check to make sure the stalls were empty. I entered the last stall, sat down on the seat and bawled my eyes out.

I didn't really like most of my teachers and I already felt like an outcast. A lot of the students in my classes were the same race as my teachers, lived in the same upscale neighborhoods as most of my teachers, went to the same churches with my teachers, and had parents that played golf or tennis at the same country club with my teachers. This led to a certain amount of perceived favoritism and sense of isolation on my part. It was bad enough that I was the token black kid in most of my classes without adding the socioeconomic disparity to the equation. My parents were just blue-collar workers trying to provide a nice home and a meager lifestyle for my brother and I. I knew people that had it worse. To my dad's credit, he was an amazing provider for his family. I just didn't fit. I wasn't rich. I wasn't poor. I was middle class in a world of extremes. I was an outspoken, non-compliant, bitter, angry black kid with a chip on her shoulder who was too smart for her own good and my teachers did not know what to do with me.

Word of my pregnancy quickly spread, from the students to the teachers to the administrators. I've never seen as much disappointment in the face of people who didn't really give a care about you anyway. My teachers would look at me with such sadness in their eyes. You would have thought I was their daughter. All of a sudden they began to say things like, "Take it easy", "You can put your head on your desk if you need to" or pat me on the back.

I had few people that I honestly thought were my friends, but for some reason, it still mattered to me what other people thought, especially when word of my pregnancy finally spread to my brother.

One afternoon, my brother came into our ranch style brick home and stormed into my bedroom. He flung a wad of twenty-dollar bills at me and said, "I know you're pregnant. Go take care of the problem." I gathered up the money, handed it to him and quietly said, "I already did." He saw the pain in my eyes. I saw the disappointment in his. He turned and closed my door and that day, I lost the boy who protected me from the world, the boy who would cook for me and make sure I was safe when my mom was too busy with her Jesus and pleasing Pastor So and So to take care of things at home. Oh, we still talked, but it was infrequent, terse and through layers of walls and hurts. A year later, he joined the army and didn't look back.

I needed a plan. I didn't want people to know that I had an abortion. It was bad enough they knew I was pregnant. I knew that Bo's blabbermouth sister, Trina, or my friend, Chris, was the culprit that put my business in the street so I started with Chris.

The next day in World History, I laid my head down on my desk, and pretended to be sick. It didn't take a lot of pretense. I was sick at heart and disgusted with myself. She asked what was wrong and how "her" baby was doing. As loud as she talked, I knew several people heard her. I could feel the heat from the glares on the back of my neck.

I turned to her with concern etched into my face and lied, well half lied, "I'm spotting pretty bad and I can't get these cramps to go away. I've taken Tylenol and everything." With a look of horror, her hands flew to her mouth, then her hands flew to the side of her head and her mouth hung open in an O. She said, in a whisper, "Are you sure?" I replied, "yeah." Turned my head and laid it back down on my desk.

For two days, I received sympathy from her and every other eye that looked my way. In those moments, I knew I could never trust Chris with another secret. As quickly as she had spread my confidential secret of pregnancy, she told the world of Dawsonville High that I had miscarried. It would have been good too, except in that small town where e'erbody know somebody who know somebody, word of my "miscarriage" reached one of Bo's older sisters who set her friend straight by informing her there was no way I could have miscarried cause Bo's daddy and brother had given him the money to give to me to have an abortion.

And so the next day, when I returned to school, I was met by a red hot, fire breathing Chris, ready to kick my ass for lying to her and stealing her sympathy when I was really a baby killer. Now that silent K that had been aflame on my chest since that cold, drizzly fall day in September was taken from its hiding place and proudly displayed front and center for all of Dawsonville High to see. And to make matters worse, on that day, Bo decided to betray me with my childhood friend, Sabrina.

After the face off with Chris, I walked down the hall to meet Bo at his locker. He and Sabrina were standing there talking. I noticed a few of the girls from Bo's neighborhood hanging off to the side looking, whispering, and looking some more. But I didn't pay them any attention. They didn't like me. I wasn't a hometown girl. My folks moved into Dawsonville two years ago from a neighboring rival small town. I'd never gotten in with the in crowd and I was okay with that. I had good friends, or so I thought.

I walked up and said hey, not thinking anything of my good friend and Bo carrying on a conversation. Bo saw me and responded by saying, "hey", but his attention was solely on Sabrina. The bell rang signaling us to our next class. He looked at her and said, "You ready?" Sabrina said yes and they walked off arm in arm. I was standing there like, "what the hell just happened?!" And Bo's friends from his neighborhood were all laughing and pointing at me like I'd been set up. With four more classes to go, I walked through the day in a fog. As if that wasn't enough, as I was leaving my last class, there they were again walking down the hall, holding hands. He was walking her to her classroom and then he leaned down and kissed her. All of my boys, the group of guys we hung out with in our junior class posse, stared at them and then stared at me. Loudly they jeered, "Oh shit! Bo, man, that is cold," and they laughed and walked away. Now, not only had her friends ridiculed and mocked me, mine had too.

With no time to find an empty bathroom stall, I walked and cried. Walked and cried. I'm not exactly sure what else happened the rest of the day. I went to work. I went home. I crawled in my bed with my work uniform on and cried myself to sleep. Aroused by a knock at the door, there stood my mom, holding the cordless telephone. I gave her a look like, "What?" "Bo," she said and handed me the phone. "What do you want?" I asked. "I need help with my Chemistry," he said. "Get Sabrina Watson to help you. Obviously, I'm not good enough," I said. "Yeah that. I like her. She's pretty. She said she'd been liking me for a long time. I think we need a break for a while." "You kissed her! You held her hand," I screamed into the phone, "You never did that with me. You said you didn't like public displays of affection! Remember that?" I was out of control with anger. "Look, he said. "I need some help with Chemistry. Are you coming over or not?" I sighed. "I'll be there in 15 minutes," I said.

I was so stupid! What was I doing? And so we went for two or three weeks, Bo with Sabrina during the day. Me in Bo's bed at night. All the while, my K was burning. I've killed my baby to keep this Negro and he could care less about me. Dumped me for my childhood friend and here I was trying to get myself pregnant by him again. And every day, the hatred would build more and more and more. The day I saw him with Sabrina was the day my heart turned cold towards him. Even though they eventually broke up and we made up, I hated him. I lived conflicted for two more years. He was my habit, like a hard drug that's difficult to say no to. I didn't want anyone else to have him, but the reality was I didn't want him myself. Even after he went off to college and I rode up and down the highway to see him. Even after spending paycheck after paycheck that I earned to outfit his dorm room, I despised him. It felt like crack. You hate what it does to you. It ruins everything, every relationship, every ounce of trust, steals your money, steals your soul and yet you keep coming back.

Bo was like that. He no longer had my heart. So why did I keep giving him my body, my energy, my time, my dimes? I don't know. Maybe in a cruel, twisted sorted of way, he was meeting the unfulfilled desire of a little girl who had always longed for affirmation, affection and attention.

Maybe somewhere deep inside, I still wanted the chance to make a different choice the next time. I had started taking the pill. I didn't want his baby. But I did want my choice again.

With Bo in college two hours away, my senior year went by in a blur. I partied. I studied. I drove up and down the interstate to see him on the weekends that I didn't work or party. Before I knew it, June 1990, had arrived and I was graduating.

My parents had been completely uninvolved in my college application process. I sought the advice of my lead high school guidance counselor. She tried to steer me to historically black colleges and universities (HBCU) only as if I wasn't good enough to handle the academic rigor of a top tier university. Pissed at the insinuation, I didn't apply to one HBCU and made it my mission to prove her and everyone else wrong about my future. So I forged my parent's name on every paper that required a parental signature, demanded my guidance counselor write application fee waiver requests for me so I didn't have to use my money to pay app fees and handled everything myself.

I applied and was accepted into Boston University, Carnegie Mellon University, Cornell University, North Carolina State University, Wake Forest University and Vanderbilt University. I'd fallen in love with Wake Forest and actually received a full scholarship to attend there.

In the back of my head, I feared my controlling mother would demand I come home every weekend since Winston Salem was such a short drive from my small town. Greatly afraid that the freedom I so desired to actually "leave" home and never return, would not be granted if I stayed in state, I chose to accept admission to Vanderbilt University.

Vanderbilt is located in Nashville, TN, and was over six hundred miles from my small town. It would take an eight to nine hour car ride for my parents to get to me or for me to get home. Our middle class income did not afford us the opportunity to fly. That was a luxury for the upper class, in my mind. Knowing this, I figured the distance was far enough to escape the clutches of my domineering mother. No one knew of my secret plan to never return home. Fear kept me from giving voice to my plan. I didn't want anything to hinder my leaving. If I was willing to kill my baby to leave this small town, I sure wasn't going to allow anything else to derail me. I didn't receive a full scholarship to Vanderbilt like I did to Wake Forest. But to me, the money I would have to pay to attend there was worth my freedom.

The transition from high school to college kind of went by in a blur. I worked two, sometimes three jobs. I liked the independence making my own money afforded me. But primarily, I worked so I didn't have to be in my parent's house a lot. On the weekends, when I wasn't working, I kicked it with high school friends or my girl, Tena. Tena and I met on the first day of Kindergarten in 1977. More like a sister than a friend, she would be, and still remains to this day, my best friend and the only childhood friend I would retain over the years.

Along the way, I met a wonderful guy name Doug. Doug was six feet tall and skinny. He had washboard abs, swimmer shoulders and the cutest tush. He wore aviator style gold rim glasses. He was dubbed the Denzel Washington look alike by all the girls, though truthfully, I never saw it. I saw Doug twice in passing, inquired about him to a mutual friend. Upon seeing him the third time, I walked into a circle of our friends interrupted the flow of the conversation, slid up to him and with a hand extended for a handshake said, "Hi, my name is Felicia. Can I have your phone number?" Completely taken aback by my boldness, Doug simply looked at me and laughed. The conversation stilled as everyone waited to see what would happen next. When he didn't offer his digits, I asked again. This made everyone laugh and he simply asked a friend very quietly, "Who is this girl?"

I let it go so I wouldn't embarrass him or myself any further. But as fate would have it, I was able to not only acquire his phone number but also where he lived. So after hours of calling and calling and getting a busy signal, I decided to drop by uninvited and knocked on his door. Using what I knew at the time would work with men, I smiled big, batted my eyelashes and he opened the door having no idea what he was in for. From that day on, Doug and I were practically inseparable.

I'd been in love with Doug for months, as best I knew love to be at eighteen years old. He didn't know it. I was afraid to tell him. History had proven that love hurts. Growing up, whenever I loved someone, they left me or misused me. So loving him frightened me because in my heart, I believed the lie that he would someday leave me or cheat on me. I kept the truth hid from Doug. I smiled. I laughed. I was falling deeper and deeper in love with him but afraid to be honest about my feelings toward him because I feared the outcome.

I easily gave my body to him, just as I had with other guys before him. But long ago, before he was even aware, I had fallen for him. We had agreed to just be friends and "kick" it. Buddies by day, lovers at night, it was the perfect combination...or so I thought. Inside of our friendship, we shared everything with each other. I'd never in my entire life shared all of me so openly and vulnerably with another person. I was a hard shell. I knew the game. I played it well. It was the way I protected myself from being rejected, abandoned, and betrayed. Fear teaches you to control, never let anyone get close enough to hurt you.

One evening, in this plutonic friendship, I sat on Doug's bed watching him get dressed for a date. To this day, I can remember what he was wearing. He had on a light denim chambray shirt and black pleated baggy dress pants, black slip on loafers, and no socks. He looked so good. I remember being sad inside that I couldn't call him my own. Not that I'd ever let him see that or know what I was really feeling. We kept up a constant dialogue as he dressed and splashed on his cologne. I watched as he took off his rings, lotioned his hands and meticulously prepared for his night out.

We took the elevator down to the lobby together. He went out the door to go on his date. I went to hang out alone at my place. An hour or so passed and my phone rang. I answered it, surprised to hear Doug's voice. "What are you doing?" he asked. I replied that I was reading. Looking at the time, I became alarmed. "What's up? I thought you were on a date. Everything okay?" I wondered why he was calling me. Doug told me that he'd been stood up and wanted to know if I was interested in going out. I said sure. We set a time to meet.

Too excited to even process that I had been his second choice, I began to ready myself for an evening out with Doug. As we approached his car, Doug came around to the passenger side and opened the car door for me which was something I'd never experienced before. We went to Darryl's restaurant. I think I ordered a salad not knowing what was appropriate to get or how much money he had. We laughed and talked about Eddie Murphy's comedy show, *RAW*, where Eddie is jonesing women who go out on dates and order salads. It was good to laugh. It was good to be with Doug. I wasn't sure exactly what the implications of this "date" meant, but I was on cloud nine. It was the first time a guy had ever taken me to a restaurant and paid for my meal. Oh, I had treated Bo Carter several times, but I always drove and I always paid. Doug made me feel like a queen. We talked and we laughed and I fell absolutely head over heels in love. I knew this was the man I wanted to be with forever. But life had taught me that there were no forevers in relationships. In fact, one of the things Doug and I shared in common is that neither of us had a desire to get married. So we maintained our comfortable plutonic arrangement of just being friends and kicking it.

A few weekends later, we ended up at the same party. I was dancing and talking to a guy at the party. As the night ended, I left the party with this guy. Doug was standing on the curb with some of his boys. As we passed by them, I waved when I saw him but inside, I felt like I had been caught. 'We were just friends, right? So technically this was okay. I mean I had to keep up my game. There was no way I could appear smitten. He was just a friend, whom I happen to be kicking it with.' A thousand small thoughts in the space of a minute flashed through my head as I willed my heart to keep beating.

In a loud, sing song voice, Doug said, "Bye Feleeecia," stretching my name out like it was a country song. The guy I was with inquired, "Is that your boy?" "No, he's just a friend," I answered. "Just a friend, uh?" the guy remarked, "No, I think that's a little bit more." I was quiet. For the first time I wondered, could Doug really like me too? I'd never seen myself as likeable, desirable. Even though Doug and I had practically been inseparable, we were just friends, right?

It would take two more defining incidents before we became exclusive. I still lived with a lot of suspicion and mistrust. I would sleep in Doug's bed with one foot on the floor just in case I needed to make a quick exit. I was always ready to run. Life had molded me into a fight or flight kind of girl and I was completely okay doing either one. My friends called me mad dog because I never smiled. I was tough as nails. I would cut you with words or with a knife, it didn't matter to me which one. As long as I protected myself and remained in control. Even in a nice, posh upper crust environment such as Vanderbilt University, I still maintained my street cred. Vanderbilt was just my ticket out of Dawsonville. I never expected it to change me or change my life.

It's amazing now to see how even on our worse day, Father God still loves us. He is still there working out things on our behalf. Looking back at the whole of my life, I see Romans 8:28, "God causes all things to work together for good to those who love God and are called according to His purpose." I can look back now and see the divine intent of His love weaving my life into a beautiful tapestry even in the worst times of my existence.

Once in college when Doug and I were dating, he made a decision to go to a party one night with some of his boys. Not just any party though. Of all the nights Doug had chosen to hang out with his boys, it would be the night of "Freak" Party. Named and modeled after Freaknik, a former annual HBCU event that took place in Atlanta, GA. This social event happened to be one where the ladies were expected to attend clad in the most scandalous and suggestive lingerie their creative, intellectual minds could conjure up. The men dressed likewise.

To his credit, Doug had never been to a Freak party and I believe he was honestly more intrigued by what people would have on and what exactly goes on at said "Freak" party. To my detriment, I allowed fear and the pain of past relationships to take me down a bad visualization trip in my mind. I conjured up Doug in his silk paisley print Victoria Secret pajama bottoms, topless with his chest all oiled up to show off his washboard abs and broad shoulders. I made myself so angry envisioning all of the girls who would come up to him and put their hands on "my man."

In my unhealed state, all I could think about was all of those college girls with their slender figures, what they would be wearing, what they would be doing or trying to do. My mind kept producing every bad scenario possible: Doug cheating on me, Doug dancing with someone else, Doug leaving me.

I was replaying the betrayal of Bo and the ridicule of being laughed at by his overt rejection of me for one of my friends. I knew the whispers on the campus wondering what Doug could possibly see in me. Or at least, I imagined that people were whispering these negative things about me because who was I to get a guy like that? In my head, I knew there were girls who would try to steal him away from me if they had the opportunity to do so. That fear triggered the need to protect myself. My friends, rage and violence, came to the rescue.

I yelled and cursed and threw things at Doug trying to bait him into a fight. Knowing that if he hit me, it would be all his fault and I could blame him and save myself the embarrassment of him rejecting me. But Doug has always been too much of a man to fall for something like that.

Realizing what I was trying to do, he threw his hands in the air and said, "Felicia, what are you doing? What is wrong with you? Where is all of this coming from?" "Go ahead and leave," I screamed, "you're just like everybody else. My momma didn't want me. Nobody wants me." "You're trippin'," Doug replied. Blowing out a breath in disgust, he shook his head and said, "I'm outta here." Still screaming with rage, I said, "Well f*** you then! Who cares? Leave. We don't need you no way. That's what everyone else does. Leave. Take your s*** and get the h*** out. Who cares?!"

All I was processing and living through in that moment was the perceived pain of rejection and betrayal and pushing Doug away before he could hurt me. Doug left our apartment on foot and began walking across Vanderbilt's campus back to his dorm room. Rage and violence, the silent partners in my head, came alive in full color saying, "Kill his ass. Hurt him. Make him pay. Don't let him treat you like s***. Everyone else has done that and got away with it. Kill him. Let him know who's in control."

Having no idea that these silent thoughts roaring through my head were being demonically inspired, I jumped in the Toyota Corolla I had borrowed from the university to do community service with and shot off across campus to find Doug. I found him near Olin Hall. I rolled down my window and began to yell at him trying to bait him once more into an argument. In a calm manner, Doug responded, "Felicia, go home." And he continued to walk away. Now I was really mad! Spurred on by rage and violence, I turned the wheels of my borrowed car towards the sidewalk and tried to run him over. Doug jumped back and said, "You're crazy as hell. We're done. I'm done with this." And he walked away.

It was like his words triggered my return to sanity. I started crying. Everything I believe to be true always comes true because I expect it to come true and it does. In fact, if I were to psychoanalyze myself, it's like I would always do something to help it come true. I was wracked with grief. I hated myself. Oh, on the outside, I acted like it didn't matter. I kept my distance from Doug and his friends. He kept his distance from me. A week passed, Doug wanted to see Brittany, our daughter that I had given birth to my second semester of college, and he needed to pick up some things from our apartment. When he came over, I was very cold; not mean but definitely distant and guarded. So was he, but I could tell he still cared for me. I think I apologized for how I behaved. He admitted the party wasn't even much fun. It was all innocent on his part.

My pain had made it so much more. I was projecting the fear and pain from my hurts with Bo and other failed relationships with boys onto my relationship with Doug. Fear breeds suspicion. Even though Doug had never given me any reason to not trust him, my fear of being rejected, abandoned, and betrayed had left me suspicious of his intentions and how he would handle himself in a situation where I wasn't there to control things.

Honestly, I don't remember all of the words that were said the day Doug walked back into our apartment, but one something he said has stuck with me some twenty-three years since. At one point in our conversation, he said, "Felicia, I'm not all those other guys. I'm Doug. I'm not going to hurt you." And for whatever reason, I absolutely believed him.

Spring semester of my sophomore year, Doug and I became engaged in the most unassuming, conversational manner a person could possibly offer a proposal in. Driving to Clarksville, TN, to visit his childhood home for the first time, Doug who is very much an internal processor made the statement in passing, "I believe I could marry you."

Having been married over twenty years, I now know that he probably had been thinking about this for days or weeks, if not months. Back then, while I knew him taking me home to see the place where he grew up was significant, I never in all of my life expected him to mention marriage.

Even though we had been exclusive for a while, we had never in anyway made that "official". It just kind of happened. So sitting there in shock, I absorbed the magnitude of his words. Here I was, nineteen years old, never wanting to be married at all, being somewhat offhandedly proposed to. So what's a girl to say? I replied, "Well, if you feel that way, let's call Pastor and talk to him about marriage counseling." And Doug responded, "OK, let's do that."

We weren't doing everything right, but at least we were going to church. In fact, much of what we were doing was wrong. We were living together, sleeping together, raising our daughter together but we weren't married. Even in the midst of all of that, Father Himself loved us.

Rom. 5:8 (NASB) But God demonstrates His own love toward us, in that while we were yet sinners, Christ died for us.

After a great visit with his mom, we went home. That night, I lay in bed wrestling with the conversation, trying to decide if I was being presumptuous. Would he change his mind? Did he really mean to say that? Had I misunderstood? All of these thoughts were going through my mind. Fear would not allow me to give voice to them. So I said nothing.

Days later, Doug announced that we should take a trip to some pawnshops in East Nashville to look at wedding rings. Still in complete disbelief that this was happening, I said a weak, "okay." Not because I didn't want to marry Doug or was having doubts, that wasn't the case at all! If I had had a picture of the man of my dreams, I'm sure he would have looked something like Doug Murrell inside and out. I just never thought I would be married. I never thought someone would truly love me enough to want to spend the rest of their life with me. In my reality, dreams meant hope and I lived with very little of that, if any at all.

My only request to Doug in regards to us getting married was that I didn't want to be a teenage bride. Adamantly opposed to being yet another statistic after already contributing to the teenage abortion statistics and the teenage mom statistics, I didn't want to give Uncle Sam another check in the societal statistic box. So in the fall of my junior year of college, approximately two weeks after my twentieth birthday, we wed.

For years, even after meeting and marrying such an incredible man, I lived out of the pain of my broken heart and bad decisions. I was hell on wheels. A rage-o-holic who kept people at bay with my loud, potty mouth and violent temper. I trusted no one and was extremely critical and judgmental.

It didn't help that violence and abuse was my normal as a child growing up with an alcoholic father. After my abortion, the rage and murderous spirit I had partnered with only grew and flourished under the generational spirits that influenced it.

In the midst of it all, my Heavenly Father loved me enough to send me the most mild tempered, loving man who saw past the dirt to the gold that lies beneath. I call him the "potential man". He's one of the few people I know that can see a pile of junk, a dilapidated house, a jacked up organization or a broken person and see the potential of success and rebuilding. And under the wings of his love and safety, for the first time in my life, I began to allow Holy Spirit permission to work on me. But transformation, at least for me, was a journey, not an overnight process.

CHAPTER 1

FACING DECEPTION
(CHOOSING PERSONAL
RESPONSIBILITY)

There were so many layers of hurt and pain, woundedness and brokenness inside my fragile soul. I had built a stronghold of deception to keep from cracking up mentally under the weight of it all. I had frozen my emotions and lived without an awareness of feeling. Being happy, peaceful or joyful were all foreign concepts to me, something for the sweet by and by but not to be experienced in this present world.

Doug and I left the world of Vanderbilt University with two children and a United States Naval commission. Off to serve his country, we headed to Newport, Rhode Island and eventually became a homesteaded military family in the Norfolk/Virginia Beach, Virginia area. We soon added two additional kids to our quiver and settled into life - kids, church, military life complete with deployments, and homeschooling. Everything was perfunctory and dutiful with no sense of passion. I lived and functioned in a nice Christian world as a church leader, homeschooling mom, officer's wife and later after Doug resigned his naval commission to go into full time vocational ministry, as a pastor's wife. If threatened, however, my friends, rage and violence, would always show up to protect me. I loved them. I was a big, badass independent free spirit with them as my friends.

Oh, I wasn't an overt rage-o-holic anymore. After all, I was a Christian! But it was there nevertheless. Like a pot on low simmering just so underneath a gas flame, it was nothing for me to slap my daughter for not getting her sight words correct during a homeschooling session or cuss someone out whom I felt had wronged me. In anger, I broke things, pounded walls, and created havoc. My inner self was in a constant state of dissatisfaction and turmoil.

I recall one day when my girls had to be at church for dance practice, we were running late and I was a ticking time bomb with frustration spilling over into rant and rage. I abhor being late and it didn't help that the girls were fined if they were late for practice. Which wasn't a good thing since we were rubbing pennies together trying to make nickels to pay bills and eke out a meager living as we "suffered" for Jesus in the pastorate.

I got every one out of the house, locked the door and closed it behind me. With all of the kids belted into the car, I started looking all around for the car keys. "Where are the keys?" I yelled, sounding demonic. The kids cowered in fear not finding a voice to answer me. So I continued to scream. Finally in a huff, I stomped around to the back of the house to peer into the window. Sure enough, there lay the car keys on the table. Because misery loves company, I tried to call my husband at work. If I was mad and suffering, in my mind, it only seemed right that he should too. Not able to reach him, I was beyond angry. I was late and I had no idea how to get into our locked home.

Ever present when I needed them, my friends, rage and violence showed up on the scene. In a fit of rage, I punched out the lower windowpane of my kitchen window with my bare fist. Cutting my fist and wrist on the shattered glass, blood streamed down my hand, I reached in to unlock the window. Too angry to even feel the pain from the glass, I stormed around to the car. I unbuckled my oldest son and demanded he come with me. I hoisted him up, put him through the now open window demanding in an angry voice that he steer clear of the broken glass and sent him inside to collect the car keys.

Keys now in hand, off I go, ready to head to the church with my bloody hand wrapped in a kitchen towel. The icing on the cake when I get in the car, I feel prompted to open the glove compartment and there in the glove compartment was the valet key. I could have easily driven to the church with the valet key, dropped the girls off at dance, picked up my husband who also had a key to our home and saved myself the $100 it cost to get the window pane repaired, a fit of rage, the fine from the dance ministry for the girls being late and the permanent scars left behind on my skin like tattoos to remind me of much angrier times.

Even then, as with the prompting to look in the glove compartment, Holy Spirit was gently showing me what it would be like to partner with Him in peace. Not that I recognized it, because my so-called friends, rage and violence were mocking me. And they would continue to show up, as needed, for several years.

As Jesus would have it, one day a friend confided in me that she felt God was punishing her for having an abortion as a teenager. Her and her husband had been trying unsuccessfully for a few years to conceive and she believed her not being able to conceive was God's punishment for her decision to terminate a pregnancy years before.

I admit to only knowing what I perceived as the negative attributes of God at the time, but one good thing I did know, God was just and He was fair. So, I told her, "I don't think you're being punished. I had an abortion as a teenager as well and I have four beautiful children today. If God was punishing you for that choice, in His fairness, He would have punished me as well." I think my logic gave her hope. But still, the pain of our tragic choices lay like walls of guilt and shame on our hearts. Hers, open and visible. Mine, as a pastor's wife, lay hidden under the façade of self-righteousness.

I mentioned that our church had a small group that was part of a national ministry called Healing Hearts and they offered a bible study, *Binding Up The Broken Hearted,* for post abortive women (Healing Hearts Ministries, 2012). I then suggested to her that we take it together.

Secretly, I had been wanting to take this bible study myself for about a year but fear of man kept me from signing up. I was too afraid of what people might say about me or about Doug, the executive pastor, if I took this class. She thought I was a hero that I would give up my time to do this with her. She had no clue that in this moment, she would be my saving grace.

At the last minute however, she had to back out. And once again, I found myself faced with a choice. So what does any good pastor's wife do? I called the leader and told her a lie. I said I might be interested in teaching something like this to women. To which she replied, "well you have to go through it as a participant before you can be considered for leadership." With that understanding, I went through the twelve-week study.

Looking back, I suspect Holy Spirit had already clued her in to how much I needed this for me and not just for others. The leader of our group shared that first night how we are all in different places in our healing process, some just coming to the realization that they needed to be operated on, some in pre-op, some on the surgeon's table in the middle of the operation, some just out of surgery and headed to post op, while some were well on their way to the process of recovery and healing. Kim, our leader, encouraged us to keep our hearts open. She said Father God would meet us in this study no matter where we were in the journey. I took her at her word and in week eight of the bible study, Father God did exactly as our leader promised.

In that week, we were to write a letter forgiving all of those who had influenced us in our decision to have an abortion. As I sat in that church classroom, writing this letter of forgiveness releasing Bo for his part in my decision, forgiving Sabrina for betraying our friendship, all of the rage and anger and violence welled up in my heart. I suddenly had a picture of the night I wanted to kill them and how often murderous thoughts would rise up within my heart creating scenario after scenario of me murdering the two of them. Honestly, if I thought that I could have killed them and gotten away with it, I would have.

I had a relative that had done time in a federal prison and one day we were allowed to visit them there and tour the facility. Listening to my relative and the other inmates share the stories of why they were there and what it was like to live on the inside, along with the vivid images of their prison cells, became the only thing that kept me from trying to carry out any acts of murder. As I sat there that night in class, I envisioned Bo and Sabrina in her Saab driving down the interstate and the car catching on fire and bursting into flames, completely burning both of them to a crisp. I was so elated they were both dead.

Embarrassed by the picture and the fact that all these years later, even after re-embracing my Christian faith, I still longed for the death of these two people who caused me so much pain and grief. My face was aflame with heat and I wanted to upend something. Frightened that the truth of who I really was would come to the surface and the other four ladies in the room would witness the eternally damned baby killer in partnership with her friends rage and violence, I quickly tried to stuff the emotions back down into my pastor's wife hat where I kept them neatly tucked away from the public eye. But no sooner had I looked up from the paper to see who might be observing this internal war that was raging so loudly did I hear a very strong, "**NO**."

So strong was the no that I thought it came from an audible source. Looking around again, I noticed that the other three ladies in the bible study were all quietly writing their letters while only the noise of the soft instrumental worship music played in the background. I didn't take time to observe what our leader was doing at the moment. Trying to compose myself, I then heard, "Jesus endured the cross for the joy that was set before Him. If you will endure this, there is joy on the other side."

So there I sat, writing with such fury that I thought I would rip my paper into shreds. Counting the cost of a loveless, consumer relationship with Bo. Reliving the betrayal of my first friend in that town, Sabrina. Drowning in the weight of Momma's rejection and lack of nurture. Feeling the loss of companionship when my brother walked out of that room. Forgiving Christina for not being the friend I could trust when I really needed a friend. Forgiving everyone that I felt should have rescued me from myself and didn't and finally forgiving myself.

Because for the first time, I had to face the truth that while it was easy to put all of the responsibility on Bo for me having an abortion, ultimately I was as responsible if not more so than he was. After all, it was my body and I alone had the final say as to the choice I made. I sobbed and sobbed and sobbed. When I was done, the worship music was still washing over the room with its peaceful tunes and I sat alone for the first time staring Truth in His face. Although I didn't yet see Him clearly, I knew He was there. Now I had the key for transformation of heart and renewing of the mind to take place.

Without coming face to face with the pain of betrayal, rejection and what that pain actually cost me, I would have continued to live inside my stronghold of deception. Every time someone hurt me, I walled myself in with another brick. Every time I was falsely accused, wronged, manipulated, controlled, rejected, abandoned, I would wall myself in. And my agreement with the lies that I believed to be true based on these experiences were like the mortar that held the bricks in place.

You know the lies: "Love hurts. No one loves me. I can never be loved. People will always use me. You can't please people. You can't trust people. Men are dogs. Men only want you for your body and your money. People always treat me like crap. Don't ever show the real you to anybody or you will get trampled on." So many lies. Every time there was a wounding, another lie bricked my walls of isolation higher and higher. My agreement with the lies cemented the bricks together sealing me in behind a wall of self-protection.

And if the walls weren't enough to defend me, I was very good at throwing a few bricks that I had stored up inside my fortress over the wall to hurt someone whenever rage or violence prompted me to do so. But in that moment, there in that room with Father, Jesus and Holy Spirit something shifted and I would never be the same. I experienced that night, in week eight of that bible study, the first crack in the fortress I had erected to protect myself from the world.

The façade that not only kept the world from getting in to hurt me had become the prison within which I voluntarily enslaved myself to rage and violence. I was a tenant in my own house and never even knew I was paying rent to deception and had relinquished self-control. Convinced that I was just sharing a room with friends when the truth all along was that rage and violence were pimping me and merely fooling me into believing that I was in charge of myself. For the very walls I had erected to protect myself were also the walls that were preventing me from receiving Father God's love into the core of my being. And without His love, I would have never known freedom.

The first leg of my journey into freedom began that night of our bible study when I took personal responsibility for my actions and owned my decision to abort my baby.

Paraphrasing Danny Silk from his book, *Keep Your Love On* (Silk, 2013), I am 100% responsible for me. Your character defects don't control my behavior. From the moment Bo had decided that abortion was the only option, I allowed myself to be controlled by his character defects. I believed the lie that others could control me. But the truth is, no one makes me. On a good day, I control myself. On a not so good day, I'm either out of control and living very reckless or choosing to allow myself to be controlled by the circumstances of life or another human being. Either way, I've chosen what form of control I experience.

Galatians 5:22-23 says, *"But the fruit of the Spirit is love, joy...self-control."* An outward sign of being internally governed by the Holy Spirit is self-control. Self-control means to master, control or restrain your desires or passions (Lexicon, 2013).

It's easy (and very common) to blame a person for your actions or your response to their actions. How often do we hear people say, "She made me mad"? But the truth is no one makes you anything. You control you. You get to choose every day how you show up.

I love how Danny describes personal responsibility (Silk, Defining The Relationship, a relationship course for those considering marriage,

2011). He says it is simply, your ability to respond. Do you have a plan? How are you going to control you when life happens to you?

At sixteen, I had no plan. It was easy to blame Bo and say "he made me kill my baby." Blame happens when I refuse to take responsibility for my personal choices. It's what Adam did to Eve in the garden, "The woman whom You gave to be with me, she gave me from the tree, and I ate."[1]

So let's ask Holy Spirit, *Holy Spirit, are there other people I have blamed for things I need to take personal responsibility for?*

If He says yes, then pray this prayer: *Holy Spirit, I repent for blaming others for things I've done wrong. I repent for abdicating my responsibility. Holy Spirit, what's the part that I am responsible for?*

Listen to what He says or shows you. Then say, *Holy Spirit, I hand you every bad decision I've made. I hand you every choice that has resulted in negative consequences for my family and me. I break agreement with any destructive stronghold that is influencing my decision to make these negative choices. Holy Spirit, what would you like to give me in exchange for these bad choices?*

Be sure to write down what He reveals to you in exchange.

Now let's ask Holy Spirit, *Holy Spirit, are there any lies I've believed that's influenced me in making negative choices?*

If He says yes, grab a pen so you can write down what He shares with you. On a sheet of paper or in a journal, write the word:

LIE:

Now ask Holy Spirit, *Holy Spirit, what are the lies I've believed?*

As He brings the lies to your mind, write them down. Once you've written down every lie He shares with you, pray this prayer: *I renounce*

---

1   Genesis 3:12

and break agreement with the lie that ...

Fill in the blank with the lies that He has revealed to you. Continue this prayer for each lie.

Then ask Holy Spirit, *What's the truth?*

Underneath the lie, write:

TRUTH:

List the truth that Holy Spirit gives you. As Holy Spirit reveals the truth to you, repeat them out loud welcoming that truth into every part of you. *I receive the truth that... into every part of me.*

e.g., I receive the truth that I am loved into every part of me. I receive the truth that I'm your son (daughter) into every part of me. I receive the truth that love heals. Love fills. Love frees. Love transforms.

CHAPTER 2

UNDERSTANDING THE PROCESS

Why do we exchange? It is my belief that God always trades up. I found this premise to be true based on Isaiah 61:3, *"To console those who mourn in Zion, To give them beauty for ashes, The oil of joy for mourning, The garment of praise for the spirit of heaviness; That they may be called trees of righteousness, The planting of the LORD, that He may be glorified."*

Even in the New Covenant, in Matthew 11:28-30, you find Jesus encouraging all who are heavy laden to come to Him and take His yoke upon them for His yoke is easy and His burden light. Here again is an example of a divine exchange. One would have to remove the heavy yoke that burdens them in order to put on Jesus' yoke. Throughout the New Covenant, you find God giving us love for fear, freedom for bondage, salvation for sin, life for death. These are all definitely upgrades of divine exchange, in my opinion.

Why do we renounce and break agreement? Renounce is an action verb that means to formally declare one's abandonment of (a claim, right, or possession) or to refuse to recognize or abide by any longer (Dictionary, 2013). When I renounce a lie, I am making a formal declaration that the power of this lie no longer has legal right to torment me or wreak havoc in my life anymore. I am refusing to agree with it or abide by it any longer. When I break something, I sever it in two and render it ineffective.

Why do we repeat the truth aloud? The Book of Genesis chronicles the creative power of life when given a voice. "Then God said...and there was." "Then God said let us make man in our image and our likeness." If God created the world with words, what do we who are made in His image create with our words? Proverbs 18:21 says, *"Death and life are in the power of the tongue."* So when I speak truth aloud, I give life to its creative nature to transform me into the truth I have spoken.

Ephesians 4:29 says, *"Let no unwholesome word proceed from your mouth, but only such a word as is good for edification according to the need of the moment, so that it will give grace to those who hear."* Repeating the truth aloud is certainly good for building up, particularly in moments of doubt, unbelief, or discouragement. In the moment that an edifying word is spoken, grace is released to those who hear it.

Why into every part of me? In Psalm 51:6, David said of the Lord, *"Behold, You desire truth in the inward parts, And in the hidden part You will make me to know wisdom."* God wants truth to permeate every part of you.

Isaiah 61:1 says, *"The Spirit of the Lord GOD is upon me, Because the LORD has anointed me To bring good news to the afflicted; He has sent me to bind up the brokenhearted, To proclaim liberty to captives And freedom to prisoners;"* The word brokenhearted in this verse is the Hebrew word, shabar. It means to break into pieces, rend violently, wreck, crush, rupture, maimed, to be shattered (Lexicon, 2013).

Often times when we experience wounding, offenses, hurts, rejection, betrayal, traumatic events or extreme levels of dysfunction, this is exactly what it feels like - crushed on every side, hard pressed, hearts completely broken. And in that place of negative emotions and pain, we create walls or parts to protect ourselves from our harsh reality. It is the desire of the Godhead to take the wounded, broken, fractured soul and bind up, sew or mend it together into a seamless tapestry of wholeness, body, soul and spirit. Francois du Toit, a South African author, writes in his book, *Divine Embrace*, "Holiness equals wholeness and seamless harmony of man's spirit, soul and body (Toit, 2012)."

CHAPTER 3

PERFORMING FOR APPROVAL

Truth is an amazing Person. The Bible says, "Jesus is the way, the Truth and the light,"[2] and that Holy Spirit is "the Spirit of Truth who will guide you into all truth."[3]

Prompted by the Holy Spirit to use week eight of that bible study as a model for doing life with God, I began to sit in the quiet of my home with instrumental worship music softly playing and I would visit with Truth. And bit-by-bit, He began to dismantle the walls of self-protection that I had bricked my heart in with and brought truth to those areas.

I realized as a little girl living in the shadow of a big brother who was dearly loved, my heart yearned for attention, affirmation and affection. I was told so many times, "you should be glad I don't believe in abortion or your tail wouldn't be here." I think my momma meant that with love in conveying her decision to keep me but what my little girl heart heard was, "I didn't want you but I didn't have a way to get rid of you." And so I grew up feeling like it was my fault that I even existed. Which in my little girl heart got translated into the lie that it's always my fault. So even though I didn't experience the attention, affirmation and affection I longed for, I truly believed it was, somehow, my fault that I didn't experience any of those things. And I ached for it; longed to be loved. I longed to be held, to be seen and to be known.

---

2   John 14:6
3   John 16:13

At the ripe old age of five, I learned how to clean well and wash the dishes to receive my mom's affirmation. My childhood brain quickly connected that while affirmation wasn't naturally given, if I performed well enough, I would receive attention and affirmation and some times maybe even affection. So I became a pleaser. If washing the dishes got me love, I'd wash the dishes. If vacuuming the floor earned me a conversation with my mom, I'd vacuum the carpet. As the years passed, instead of affirmation, I received a backhand or the belt from a harsh taskmaster who could never be pleased. What did life teach my little adolescent heart? You'll never be able to please people. You can't do anything right. If you perform well, you'll be loved. If you don't, you will be punished. Love hurts. It's always your fault. You're not worth talking to. No one wants to listen to you. No one wants you around. No one has time for you. You should have never been born. No one wants you. No one loves you.

Holy Spirit once spoke this truth into my heart, He said, "Felicia, in the absence of relationship the only way to be known is through performance." Relationships take time and intentionality. It is an investment to know the real you, see the real you, hear the real you. It is the vulnerable, authentic sharing of one's self with another. Wm. Paul Young pens it best in his book, *The Shack*, "Life takes a bit of time and a lot of relationship."

There are many more people in the world like the five year old me whose hearts are crying out, "All I really want is to be loved. All I really want is to be known." To be known is to be loved. To be loved is to be known. And the worse thing in the world is for someone to not know you. We were created for love. We were created for fellowship. Often, in the absence of people taking the time to get to know us, what our orphaned hearts do is make a decision to perform so we will be seen. Hoping that drawing the attention of man will also draw the love and acceptance of man.

Serving and doing for others in and of itself is a noble and charitable thing. The issue is the state of our heart. Are we doing this out of love or because we are trying to find love, find acceptance? As a five year old washing the dishes and vacuuming the carpet, I was totally performing because I was trying to "make" my mom love me, "make" my mom see me, "make" my mom want to be with me. How many religious acts do we perform trying to "make" God happy with us? God doesn't want us trapped on the hamster wheel of performance always wondering if we're doing enough and how much is enough. The truth is, He has always loved us.

The truth is we don't have to do to catch His eye, to win over His approval or affection. We've always had it.

John 16:27 The Father Himself loves you.

Isaiah 43:4 Since you were precious in My sight, You have been honored, And I have loved you;

Jeremiah 31:3 The LORD has appeared of old to me, [saying]: "Yes, I have loved you with an everlasting love; Therefore with loving kindness I have drawn you."

Malachi 1:2 "I have loved you," says the LORD.

*John 13:34 "A new commandment I give to you, that you love one another; as **I have loved you.**"*

John 15:9 As the Father loved Me, I also have loved you; abide in My love.

Performance is a counterfeit and was never meant to achieve the acceptance, affirmation, and affection one receives in an intimate relationship with God or another human being.

So let's ask Holy Spirit, *Holy Spirit, are there areas in my life where I have performed for love?*

If He says yes, I want you to ask Holy Spirit this question.

Holy Spirit, when was the first time I believed the lie that love could be obtained through performance?

You may have recalled a memory from your childhood or some time in your past when you first began to believe this lie, a quick snapshot of an incident flashing through your mind. If that memory includes other people, you need to forgive them for influencing you in believing this lie.

Holy Spirit, I renounce and break agreement with the lie that love can be obtained through performance. I repent for agreeing with this lie and allowing it to influence my life. I forgive myself for participating with this lie and I forgive (insert name or names here) for influencing me in this ungodly belief. Holy Spirit, are there any more lies I've believed about performance?

If you didn't recall a childhood memory or something from your past, it is completely okay. The idea here is not to conjure up something or even dig around for an issue. If there's something there that Father wants to deal with, trust the Holy Spirit to bring it to your remembrance.

Listen closely to what He says. If He says yes, grab a pen so you can write down what He shares with you. On a sheet of paper or in your journal, write the word:

LIE:

Now ask Holy Spirit, *Holy Spirit, what are the lies I've believed?*

As He brings the lies to your mind, write them down. Once you've written down every lie He shares with you, pray this prayer: *I renounce and break agreement with the lie that ...*

Fill in the blank with the lies that He has revealed to you. Continue this prayer for each lie.

Then ask Holy Spirit, *What's the truth You want me to believe?*

Underneath the lie, write:

TRUTH:

List the truth that Holy Spirit gives you.

Finally, ask Holy Spirit, *Holy Spirit, what does it look like to live in an intimate relationship with You that is free of performance?*

Be sure to write down what He tells you. You'll want to return to that truth over and over again until it becomes a part of you.

CHAPTER 4

GETTING FREE FROM
THE CONSTRAINTS OF CONTROL

My kids are the most jovial people I know. They are so full of life, so full of laughter and just really know how to have fun. Our home is full of freedom and their lives reflect that.

Once, we visited someone who tends to have a very controlling personality. I watched in utter amazement at the effects of control on my three vivacious teens. They withered under this person's hand. They were withdrawn. They didn't want to talk aloud because doing so seemed to give this person ammunition to use against them. They sat staring at the TV, completely uncomfortable, ready to be set free from the controlling figure.

Shortly after our time in the presence of this person, we left their home to go visit someone else. This person happens to embrace an honoring lifestyle that is full of love and freedom. I was amazed to see my kids go from night to day in the presence of these two people. They were once again animated, talkative, laughing, full of love, touching, embracing. It was such a contrast in behavior in such a short amount of time that I began to ponder why the stark difference. If growth happens as a result of evaluated experiences, I wanted to look at this, in light of my kids' behavior in these two contrasting environments with intentionality to understand myself, where I've been and where I'm going.

Admittedly, I come from a history of strong, opinionated black women, both paternally and maternally. Unfortunately, because of that, I've had lots of experience controlling and being controlled. Fortunately for my family, I had an amazing encounter with the Heavenly Father's love that completely set me free. In complete transparency, I admit that it's a constant dialogue with myself and with Holy Spirit when things scare me not to go back and pick up control.

As I began to understand my experience with control, I was taken back to the Garden of Eden, where the Lord placed Adam and Eve and walked with them in the cool of the day. In this garden, the Lord placed several trees, but two trees from the garden are mentioned specifically in scripture by name – the tree of life and the tree of the knowledge of good and evil. From the onset, the Lord commanded Adam to eat of everything in the garden except the Tree of the Knowledge of Good and Evil.[4]

I find it interesting that Adam was given complete stewardship of the garden. He was free to do whatever he pleased, whenever he pleased as if he owned it all. The only command he was to follow was to not eat of the tree of the knowledge of good and evil. In this garden, he had so many options. Everything was available to him. He was free to pick and choose from whatever he wanted.

Interesting thing about freedom, freedom is full of options but it's up to us to manage our choices wisely. Galatians 5:1 says, *"It was for freedom that Christ set us free; therefore keep standing firm and do not be subject again to a yoke of slavery."* For Adam, really for all mankind, the day he ate of the tree of the knowledge of good and evil, his life changed. Our life changed. As a result of his disobedience to God's instructions, the human race was introduced to control.

The primary definition of control is to exercise restraint or direction over; dominate; command (Dictionary, 2013). In Genesis 3:16, Eve was told that Adam would rule over or dominate her. Then we see God exercising restraint when He placed Adam and Eve out of the Garden

---

4   Genesis 2:16-17

and put an angel in front of the way to the tree of life to guard them from finding their way back to it.[5] In Adam's partaking of the fruit from the Tree of the Knowledge of Good and Evil, his life was reduced from limitless options and an eternal life of freedom to a life of boundaries, restraints, constraints, bondage and oppression. For the first time ever, he went from resting and walking with God to working and toiling in the absence of a Father. He, and all of us along with him, went from being a son to being an orphan.

Control reduces a person to life inside of someone else's expectations for them. When you are free, you have permission to be who you want to be, to explore, to dream, to live. Control strips a person of their voice, as the only opinion that matters is that of the one with all the power. When you are free, you have permission to say what's on your heart, share your dreams, give names and meaning to things. Control confines a person to the walls of someone else's box and limits how far you can go, keeping you within the boundaries of your controller's reigns. When you are free, there are no boundaries. Love sets the limits. Only you control you when you are free. Only you determine how far you'll go and where you'll stop. When you are free, you can have as much of God as you want because there is no end to Him. His goodness knows no bounds. His love never ends. He goes on and on. When you are being controlled, there is no need to use your brain because someone else does all of your thinking for you. When you're free, you are empowered to think for yourself. You are free to choose, free to decide.

I love Psalm 32:8, *"I will instruct you and teach you in the way you should go; I will guide you with my eye."* I imagine that's how life was for Adam before the fall. Father God instructing and teaching him. Adam looking into Father's eyes of love and seeing a reflection of himself, seeing his destiny, seeing his purpose, understanding his identity, seeing Father's acceptance and great love for him. I imagine that fateful day when he hid himself in the garden, he did so not only because he realized he had chosen wrong, but also because he was afraid of the disappointment and disapproval he might see in his Father's eyes.

---

5   Genesis 3:23-24

For years, I was taught that God couldn't look on sin. The faulty teaching creates a theology of separation and produces a striving in the heart of man to somehow make their way back to God. What a powerful revelation for me the first day I read Genesis 3:8-9 and realized that God didn't hide Himself or turn Himself away from Adam after he sinned. In fact, He did the opposite. He pursued Adam. Walking through the garden in the cool of the day, He calls out to Adam, "Where are you?"

But the day that Adam ate the fruit from the tree of the knowledge of good and evil was also the first time an emotion outside of love was experienced by man. Genesis 3:10, Adam said to God, *"I was afraid...so I hid myself."* In our fear, we believe the worse about those who love and care for us. In our fear, we hide ourselves from love.

The love that we see in our Father's eyes causes us to abound in freedom. It keeps our hearts connected and releases us to live full on enjoying the freedom for which Christ has set us free. When control is all you've known, freedom can be really scary. If only I am controlling me, that means only I can take responsibility for me and I no longer have someone else to blame for my failures, my mistakes, and my bad choices.

"But the fruit of the Spirit is love, joy, peace, patience, kindness, goodness, faithfulness, gentleness, self-control; against such things there is no law."[6] Fruit is produced as a result of intimacy. Because my Heavenly Father loves me and I love Him, I choose to control myself and restrain myself from doing anything that would break His heart and cause a disconnect in our intimacy. I look in His eyes and see His great love for me and it guides me to make decisions that protect our relationship.

1 John 4:18 says, *"Perfect love casts out fear. There is no fear in love because fear involves punishment."* Often times, people resort to control because they are afraid. Their fear of how a person or situation will turn out causes them to exert their power over another. I realized this as I evaluated the experience of my kids in the presence of that controlling person. Much of what governs them is fear and because of it, they use

---

6   Galatians 5:22-23

control to keep things and people in order.

When love is present, fear is not and thus the need to control someone or something does not exist. I trust that my love for that person and their reciprocating love for me is enough. This was the experience my children had in the second home we visited that day. Under a fearful, controlling environment, they withered and withdrew. In a loving environment, they flourished and came alive.

This is why Christ died. This is freedom: to live in relationship with Father, Son, and Holy Spirit walking with them in the cool of the day; to live in relationship with one another;[7] to be fruitful and multiply; to rule over the earth and subdue;[8] to partner with God in life ruling over every living thing.[9] The day Adam ate that fruit he lost his sonship, not only his but ours as well. This is why Christ died, to restore to us all that Adam lost. Freedom is glorious. Christ came to restore the glory that Adam lost on that fateful day.[10] I will not leave you as orphans, I will come to you.[11]

Grace and truth is realized through Jesus Christ.[12] You shall know the truth, and the truth shall make you free.[13] Truth makes you free. Grace, God's divine enablement, sustains you and allows you to live in freedom. Therefore if the Son makes you free, you are free indeed.[14] For the law of the Spirit of life in Christ Jesus has made you free from the law of sin and death.[15]

This freedom exists for all who have called on the name of the Lord Jesus Christ as their personal Savior. Unfortunately, many remain just on the other side of the door of the Kingdom scared to explore the vast riches and glory of the land called freedom. There is an old African tale

---

7   Genesis 2:18
8   Genesis 1:28
9   Genesis 1:28
10   Romans 3:23
11   John 14:18
12   John 1:17
13   John 8:32
14   John 8:36
15   Romans 8:2

about an elephant that was ensnared at birth and grew up with a chain around one ankle to keep him from running off. As the elephant grew, he broke the chain on his ankle. The owner however, never needed to replace the chain. No longer bound physically, the elephant remained mentally in captivity long after the chain had been removed. Many live like that. Through Jesus' death on the cross, their glory has been restored. They have a voice. They've been empowered to think. They have been set free for freedom and yet mentally, they remain a captive, a powerless victim never fully enjoying all that life and the Kingdom of God have to offer.

I grew up this way. I had no voice. Someone else did all of my thinking for me. Someone else made all of my decisions for me. Someone else set the rules for me and mapped out my life's plan. Like a naughty puppy, I was afraid to look at God full on because I expected to see the same disappointment mirrored in His eyes that I so often saw in the eyes of my controllers. After years of being controlled, I grew tired of it and fought back the only way I knew how: rebellion, anger, rage. I bucked the rules. I tried to turn my back on all that I knew. Then I had a child and repeated the cycle on her.

People who control or have been controlled preach a God of control because control is all they know. Control was all I knew. Even in trying to deepen my faith, I still remained aloof with God, as I never had quite resolved the control thing. And though I needed the fire insurance to secure my residence for life after death, I wasn't so sure how much I really liked interacting with a controlling God, as it had never quite worked out in my favor any other time. It seemed like the score was always, Controller 1 Felicia 0. Instead of relationship, I sought to deepen my faith through performance, volunteering, serving in the church – something akin to penance. I was trying to earn something that had already been freely provided for me.

Then one day, someone introduced me to a Father in Heaven who loved me; a Father who was proud of me, pleased me with, delighted in me; a Father whose eyes beam with approval. I remember sensing His presence and hearing Him gently persuade me to look at Him. I remember my reluctance to do so. Finally, hesitantly, I lifted my face to look in His and to my amazement; I saw nothing but pure LOVE flowing through His eyes. It looked like oceans and felt like warm, ooey gooey liquid fire running through me. I was wrecked and I've never been the same since that day. I found myself, find myself, going back often to His face, to look in His eyes. And looking for the first time into His face and realizing there wasn't any disappointment or disillusionment there, I had to wonder, what would have happened if instead of hiding Adam had ran to Him, looked in His eyes, seen His great love for mankind and asked forgiveness? We'll never know. Fear clouded the way Adam perceived God as if he was looking through a glass darkly. But the truth is, even before Adam was, Father God already had our destiny in mind for the lamb had already been slain.[16]

His eyes define me, guide me, woo me, approve me. His eyes of love have released me into my destiny, a land of freedom, a land of limitless options. His grace sustains me and as I receive His grace, I'm learning how to navigate this wonderful life of freedom. I'm finding my voice again. I love to tell of His goodness, sing of His wonders. I'm having my own thoughts. I'm living without boundaries within the confines of His love. I'm empowered to be me, the me He created me to be.

Evaluating this experience, I surmise that freedom is life. Freedom is being. Freedom is freeing.

What about you? Has fear colored your perspective of God? Are there people who have controlled you? People who have stolen your voice? Exerted their opinion above your own?

Have you truly experienced the glorious freedom of being a son (daughter) of God? Would you like to?

I invite you to pray with me: *I renounce and break agreement with the lie that I have to hide myself from God. I renounce and break agreement with the lie that others can control me. I renounce and break agreement with the lie that I can control other people. Holy Spirit, what other lies*

---

16   Ephesians 1:4; Revelation 13:8

have I believed that may be preventing me from experiencing the glorious freedom of being your son (daughter)?

What's the truth you want me to believe?

Be sure to record the truth that Holy Spirit gives you.

The Bible says in Luke 11:34, *The eye is the lamp of your body; when your eye is clear, your whole body also is full of light; but when it is bad, your body also is full of darkness.*

So let's make sure we are seeing clearly. Let's ask Holy Spirit: *Holy Spirit, how has fear clouded my perspective of Father God?*

Be sure to record what He says. Then ask:

Holy Spirit, have I allowed others to control me?

If He says yes, let's ask Him: *Holy Spirit, is there anyone specifically that I need to forgive for controlling me?*

As He brings the person or people to mind, I encourage you to pray this prayer: _____, *I forgive you for controlling me. I forgive you for stealing my voice and pulling my life along as if I were a puppet being manipulated by your strings. I break every ungodly and unhealthy soul tie between you and I. And I sever your control from ruling over me. I give back to you every part of you and I take back to me every part of me, washed through the blood of Jesus. Holy Spirit, what specifically do I need to take back?*

CHAPTER 5

DEALING WITH MOTHER WOUNDS

For me, my mom was always the synonym of control. But one day, as I sat with Truth, I began to peer through a lens that offered a different view of her. And this time, I saw a woman that had been hurt herself, scarred by life, launched into a life created by her own choices that had she chosen differently, more wisely, would have looked different from the one she created. And I forgave that hurting young woman who is my mom. I forgave her for everything her lack of affirmation, affection, and attention cost me. I forgave her for not being able to provide me with comfort, direction, nurture or guidance. I forgave her for not being able to love me the way I needed or wanted to be loved. I forgave her for every beating, every bruise, every time I was hit out of her frustration and anger. I forgave her for not knowing how to be affectionate towards me, for not being able to express love to me in a way that I could hear it and receive it. I forgave her for not being able to show me that I was wanted. I forgave her for controlling and manipulating me, dominating my life. I forgave her for not taking the time to see me, to hear me or know me. I forgave her for the things she wrongly assumed or presumed to know about me. I forgave her for caring more about the church than she did for me. And more bricks fell from my stronghold of deception as Truth shined its light on my past.

In forgiving my mom, I took the hook out of my heart that was binding me to her. In forgiving her, I chose to let the guilty go free. I released her from ever owing me for her past failures. My forgiveness says, "Mom, I no longer want to make you pay for what you did to me." In forgiving my mom, I tore up the note that demanded repayment for the debt. I also had to ask Holy Spirit to come alongside me and pull up the bitterroot judgment I had formed in my heart towards my mom. You see every time I referred to my mom as controlling, domineering, hyper religious or all those terms I gave for her character defects, in essence, I was exalting my opinion of my mom above how God sees her and I was passing judgment. Until we repent and break agreement, judgments will always reproduce negative repeating patterns.

In forgiving my mom, I no longer choose to look at her through the lens of my pain. I've taken all of my pain, all of those lies, all of the injured expectations, all of that rejection and betrayal that I felt and I've handed it to Jesus. This is what He died for, all of that was nailed to the cross with Him. I no longer have to carry around a burden that He's already paid for. In forgiving my mom, my eye became clearer.

And that little five year old girl that had been walled off in my brick palace of self protection was now free to go be with Father God to receive His love, identity and protection. Father God came into my heart and filled the parental love deficit of that frightened little girl and loved her so fully that it sealed the leaks that riddled the love container of my soul filling every void that was starving for affirmation, acceptance and affection.

Do you need to forgive your mom? Perhaps like me, your mom failed to love you the way you needed to be loved. Failed to accurately re-present the Motherheart of God to you.

The heart of the Father is always reconciliation and restoration.

2 Cor. 5:19(NASB), *"...namely, that God was in Christ reconciling the world to Himself, not counting their trespasses against them, and He has committed to us the word of reconciliation."* Not only does He not count the sins of others against them, He wants us to be just like Him and do the same.

Unforgiveness says you are guilty on all counts for the charges against you and I demand you pay for your wrong deeds. But the truth is, on that day more than 2000 years ago, Jesus died for every sin and He died for every incorrect, sinful response to those sins. He's canceled the debt and absorbed the loss for the sins of the victim and the sins of the perpetrator. When we don't forgive, we are trying to make someone pay again for something that's already been settled and reconciled and that's fraud.

Now let's get real...as Christians, we have learned to forgive from our will as a deliberate act or choice. Forgiving someone from the heart includes counting the cost of what has been stolen from you by that transgression or violation that was perpetrated against you. It's more than just I forgive you for the act. That act has layers of consequences and effects underneath it. For me with my mom, her lack of love and nurture cost me the ability to give love and nurture to my kids because I had no clue what that looked like. Her control cost me the ability to learn how to manage myself, think for myself. Her not knowing me cost me the friendship of a mom as I grew up. It cost me my ability to trust and love freely. The lies we agree with when someone wrongs us lead us to perform or live out of those painful experiences. It creates a false reality. In order to completely let my mom off the hook, I had to evaluate the experience with Holy Spirit, count the cost, sum it all up, then choose to forgive her and hand the pain of the experience to Jesus. If not, I would find myself repeatedly mad and on guard each time I came in contact with her or in an experience that reminded me of her.

If you have searched the whole of your personal relationship with your mother and found her guilty in any way, I'd like to invite you to pray this prayer aloud:

Mom, you wronged me. You hurt me. I have counted the cost. I recognize what I loss by your sins against me. I am fully aware of the pain, the agony, the rejection, the betrayal, the hurt, the abandonment, the insecurity, every negative emotion your sins have cost me. But today, in the face of all of that, I choose to allow you, the guilty, to go free. And in so doing, I take the hook out of my heart that binds me to your trespasses and I tear up every IOU that I am holding against you. Mom, you owe me nothing. You don't owe me an apology, an explanation, a change for the better, nothing. My forgiving you isn't conditional on what you do or don't do. Mom, I forgive you from my heart because Jesus has already forgiven you. To hold you guilty any longer is spiritual fraud because I would be demanding that you pay for something Jesus' death on the cross has settled and reconciled. So, Mom, today I am choosing to be like Jesus and have a heart that forgives. I forgive you for everything you've ever done wrong to me, knowingly and unknowingly. I repent for judging you. I ask you to forgive me for exalting my opinion of you above Father God's opinion of you. I break agreement with every lie I've believed to be true about you. I release you, Mom. And I bless you to be the woman of God that He has created you to be.

Now let's ask Holy Spirit: *Holy Spirit, what lies have I believed to be true about my Mom?*

Listen closely to what He says. If He reveals any lies to you, grab a pen so you can write them down. On a sheet of paper, write the word:

LIE:

Once you've written down every lie He shares with you, pray this prayer: *I renounce and break agreement with the lie that...*

Fill in the blank with the lies that He has revealed to you. Continue this prayer for each lie.

Then ask Holy Spirit, *What's the truth about my Mom?*

Underneath the lie, write:

TRUTH:

List the truth that Holy Spirit gives you.

When we have been wounded, the pain, trauma, offense, or hurt that we bear as a result of those wounds cause us to see people differently. When our hearts are healed, Holy Spirit can come alongside as the Spirit of Truth and give us a right perspective of the person that has hurt us. Only He can change the lens through which we see Him, other people, our circumstances and ourselves.

Matthew 6:22(NASB) The eye is the lamp of the body; so then if your eye is clear, your whole body will be full of light.

Finally, ask Holy Spirit these two questions and be sure to record your answers:

Holy Spirit, how do you see my mother?

Holy Spirit, how do you want ME to see my mother?

CHAPTER 6

TRAPPED IN A CYCLE
OF SEXUAL SINS

All of my girl cousins on my mother's side that I hung out with were two to four years older than me. This meant, whenever I spent the night at their homes or was hanging out with them and their friends, I was placing myself in social settings were the crowd was hormonally more mature than I. I'd always been an "old soul" or at least my great grandmother (Big Grandma) thought so.

I was somewhat of a chameleon in my character and had a great knack for sizing up a room and fitting in. With as much dysfunction that existed in our home, I had learned very early to be adaptable. And as genetics would have it, I was very developed for a twelve year old girl at least in the areas that would catch the eye of a teenage boy going through puberty.

With the absence of authentic relationships and the generational spirit of sexual immorality there to influence me in the area of fornication and promiscuity, I found myself living a horrendous reality that has existed throughout the ages. Girls give sex for love. Boys give love for sex.

So as a young girl at the age of twelve, still in search of affirmation, affection, and attention, I started giving myself away to boys and very easily came into agreement with the lies that, "If you give someone what they want, they will give you what you want. If you want to be loved, sex is the way to get it." Buying into these lies, I went from partner to partner to partner trying to get my love tank filled only to be handed more bricks and mortar from every relationship that ended in betrayal, rejection or abandonment. Angry and disillusioned at myself, my heart was the evil one's playground. I believed his lies that I was no good. That no one wanted me. That I would never amount to anything. That I was only good for the back seat. That rejection, abandonment and betrayal would be a common occurrence in my life. I believed his lies that I was filthy, dirty, cheap, easy, unloved, and unwanted. And his lies became my identity. Covered in a cloak of false labels, I hated myself and didn't even know it.

I'd "fall in love" with a guy only to find out that while my body was good enough for him, I wasn't pretty enough to be seen in public with him. I believed the lie that I was ugly. I would always be rejected. I mean if my own momma didn't want me, why would any boy want me? So when Bo Carter came around, pursuing me, wanting to hook up with me, the little girl in me who was longing to be loved, longing to be affirmed was enamored that this star athlete would seek me out. And yet, it was these very lies that fed into my decision to stay with him for a number of years.

It was a pattern I was use to. One that I had told myself was the truth. After all, every experience up to that point had only confirmed the truth of the lies I believed. Rejection, betrayal, abandonment, lack of affection was my normal. Why should I have expected anything different? These things were so familiar to me. I had no idea life wasn't meant to be lived this way.

Somewhere in the last two weeks of our post abortive bible study, it struck me that I really didn't know who I was. We were learning about soul ties and how when you give yourself sexually to someone a little piece of them is left with you and a little piece of you is left with them.

In more recent times, I've heard this analogy to describe this spiritual transaction. Imagine taking two wood boards and gluing them together with wood glue, allowing the glue to dry thereby cementing the boards to one another. After a period of time, someone or something comes along and rips the two boards apart. When the boards are separated, each board still has particle pieces of the other board glued to its surface, a visible and lasting testimony that two had once been joined. Now, imagine what happens when I take these two ripped apart boards and join them with wood glue to two other boards and after a time repeat the process of ripping those newly joined boards together. Now the original two boards not only have some of the particles from their experience of being joined together on their surface, they have added the residue of being joined to new boards and then being ripped apart from those boards.

Soul ties are exactly like this. Imagine being extremely promiscuous and having this ripping apart analogy happen to you multiple times. Not only that, compound that with that fact that you are being promiscuous with other people who most likely are being promiscuous so not only are you getting pieces of their soul in this joining together, you are also getting bits and pieces of every person they have been with sexually and you are giving to them bits and pieces of every person you have ever been with sexually. It's easy to see how you could become so covered with bits and pieces of others that you eventually lose who you actually are in the process.

In that homework exercise for my post abortive bible study, I admitted to God that I could be anything anyone wanted or needed me to be but I had absolutely no idea as to who I really was.

Over a series of quiet times, Holy Spirit graciously began to bring to my remembrance the boys that I had given myself to. Each time he would bring up a memory, I would forgive that young boy for taking advantage of me or forgive myself for taking advantage of them. I would forgive myself for participating and agreeing with sexual sin and I would break every ungodly and unhealthy soul tie between that individual and I. Once we were done, I knew that the door to sexual sin was forever closed.

For me, I had found the love of my life and said yes to him. I wasn't concerned about sinning against Doug. I wanted to sever the influence of that generational spirit that had perpetuated sexual immorality throughout my family line. I wanted to break the curses that caused a history of teenage pregnancy and a devaluing of marriage in our family all generations back and all generations forward.

I celebrated enthusiastically when each one of my children passed the age of twelve and hadn't given themselves away sexually. I celebrated again when my girls reached sixteen and hadn't become pregnant. These milestones were like stones of remembrance for me. I could look at each one and celebrate the faithfulness of a God who can so completely change the DNA and lineage of one's family line. Years of living under a curse could be completely eradicated by the blessing of a father. We were seeing the fruit of the Father's blessing.

Have you seen the destruction of sexual sin in your own life? Would you like to see that door closed? If you have ever participated in fornication, pornography, lewdness, homosexuality, adultery, bestiality, molestation, or rape, I invite you to pray this prayer with me.

Jesus, I repent for my sins and my ancestors' sins in the area of sexual immorality. I repent for all the ways I have agreed with this sin knowingly or unknowingly. I break all agreements with any generational spirits that have influenced me to participate and agree with sexual immorality. I sever my agreement with sexual sin. Sexual sin, I nail you to the cross of Jesus. He died so I would no longer be plagued or tempted by you.

If promiscuity has been an issue for you, ask Holy Spirit: *Holy Spirit, what is the childhood lie I believed that caused me to give myself away so freely?*

Holy Spirit, what are the lies I've believed that has kept the door to sexual sin open in my heart?

On a sheet of paper or in your journal, write the word:

LIE:

Once you've written down every lie He shares with you, pray this prayer:

I renounce and break agreement with the lie that... Holy Spirit, drain that lie out of me and every thing that came with it.

Fill in the blank with the lies that He has revealed to you. Continue this prayer for each lie.

Then ask Holy Spirit, *What's the truth?*

Underneath the lie, write:

TRUTH:

List the truth that Holy Spirit gives you. As Holy Spirit reveals the truth to you, repeat them out loud welcoming that truth into every part of you.

I receive the truth that... into every part of me.

Holy Spirit, is there anyone I need to forgive for influencing me to participate with sexual immorality?

Listen to what He says or shows you.

If He brings people to mind say: _____ *I forgive you for influencing me in the area of sexual sin. I forgive you for...* (Be specific about the things you need to forgive them for.)

Now, let's get rid of the soul ties that bind you spiritually and emotionally to your former partners.

Pray this prayer: *I break every ungodly and unhealthy soul tie between me and* (name your sexual partner). *I give back to him/her every part of him/her and I take back to me every part of me washed through the blood of Jesus.*

Pause for a moment and think about what was stolen from you or what you gave away in that sexual encounter and/or in that relationship with that person.

Then continue with the prayer:

I take back … (i.e., I take back my voice, I take back my innocence, I take my virtue, I take back my purity, I take back my right to give myself to whom I want to give myself to…)

Holy Spirit, what else do I need to take back?

After you have taken back everything that was stolen or wrongly given away. Continue the prayer:

I cut the ties that bind me to you and I release you in Jesus name.

Once you have severed all of your soul ties, invite Jesus to come and close the door to sexual sin.

Jesus, would you come and close the door to sexual sin?

See if you can picture this door being closed in your mind's eye. If the door closes completely, ask Jesus to seal the door with His blood.

Jesus, would you come and seal this door completely shut with Your blood?

If you can't picture the door being completely closed, I encourage you to ask Holy Spirit if there are any more lies that is preventing this door from closing.

Final Question: *Holy Spirit, what does self-control look like for me?*

Be sure to write down what He says.

CHAPTER 7

THE POWER OF AGREEMENT: EXCHANGING LIES FOR TRUTH

What comes along with lies? The demonic traffics in lies. John 8:44 says, *"You are of your father the devil, and you want to do the desires of your father. He was a murderer from the beginning, and does not stand in the truth because there is no truth in him. Whenever he speaks a lie, he speaks from his own nature, for he is a liar and the father of lies."* When we agree with the evil one's lies, it opens the door for him to bring demonic torment. While this is not always the case, in asking Holy Spirit to empty your heart and soul of the lies you've believed and to remove anything else that has attached itself to you as a result of those lies, we give ourselves a spiritual cleansing and cut off any demonic influence that may have resulted.

Our agreement with lies is like the mortar that cements bricks together. Our agreement allows the lies to build demonic structures or strongholds within our hearts. When we break agreement with the lies, there is nothing to hold the stronghold together. Thus allowing the demonic structure to collapse. Often people will break agreement with the lies, but they won't fully embrace the truth. That is because they have believed a lie for so long that Holy Spirit's truth sounds foreign at first.

I've heard Bill Johnson, senior leader of Bethel Church in Redding, CA, say, "You know how banks teach tellers to identify counterfeit money? They lock them in a room and have them study the real thing." Think on that. When we become so familiar with truth, we will easily identify something as a lie. It will just stand out as odd, different. So, you are going to need to study your truth. This is why I've encouraged you along the way to record your truths. The power of life and death is in the tongue. If you don't receive your truth into every part of you, if you fail to give life to your truth by verbally declaring it over yourself, it will die. It doesn't change it from being true, it just nullifies the effect of that truth over you if you choose not to embrace it. The truth needs to become so much a part of you that you and Truth become one. What happens when we fail to appropriate truth into our souls in such manner?

We find the answer in Matthew 12:43-45, *"Now when the unclean spirit goes out of a man, it passes through waterless places seeking rest, and does not find it. Then it says, 'I will return to my house from which I came'; and when it comes, it finds it unoccupied, swept, and put in order. Then it goes and takes along with it seven other spirits more wicked than itself, and they go in and live there; and the last state of that man becomes worse than the first."*

When we break agreement with lies, it's like having our house cleaned. If we don't replace the lies with truth, our souls remain empty. The Bible says those unclean spirits will return with 'friends'. I know they are not really "friends". I am being facetious in my word choice but there is something key in there, I believe we often miss. It does say, the unclean spirit will return. Just because the enemy tries to feed you those lies again doesn't mean you have to agree with them. You can tell him NO and declare the truth. However, if you don't familiarize yourself with truth, those old stinky counterfeit lies won't stand out as odd or foreign. You will embrace that familiar spirit as if the thought originated in your own head.

The process of remaining free after being set free from the bondage of lies is one of cultivation. If I only prep the soil of my heart by removing the lies, wounds, fear, bitterness, offenses and pains of the past but never cultivate a vibrant life of truth, love, hope, peace, expectancy, and trust, eventually the weeds will return and the state of my heart will be worse than it was before. Cultivating truth expands the borders of freedom within your heart and soul. So go ahead and plant good stuff! Truth flourishes in the soil of love.

CHAPTER 8

THE VALUE OF SELF WORTH

Sitting down with Truth one day, He showed me that I would always give away freely what I deemed to be cheap. If I had no value for myself, I would not honor the treasure I was. "Felicia," Holy Spirit said, "you're a diamond but you see yourself as a cubic zirconium. You won't have the same appreciation or value for a cubic zirconium, as you will for a diamond."

Think about a ring that has a cubic zirconium stone. You'll take that five dollar ring off and sit it down anywhere. You won't protect it with the same zeal that you would a five thousand dollar diamond. You don't care if it gets lost or bent. You won't even think twice about giving it away to someone else. After all, it was just five dollars. So easily discarded because of its lack of value. Carelessly tossed aside with little thought or attention. A one carat, clear cut diamond ring on the other hand, it's going to be cleaned on a regular basis, stored in its jewelry case at night, removed when mixing dough or meatloaf so nothing muddies the clarity of the stone. And yet, even in the removal, one eye is always on the stone with knowledge of its whereabouts at all times. It won't be so easily given to a stranger or tossed aside.

"Felicia," Holy Spirit continued, "it's imperative that you understand the value of what you're worth. You must see yourself and come into agreement with how I see you. If you understood your value, you wouldn't give yourself away so cheaply."

While I knew in my spirit that what Holy Spirit was saying was true, my heart couldn't allow myself to believe that it was true. I had done so many bad things. There was no way I was valuable. Can you hear the lies mocking Truth? "You're worthless. You're insignificant. You're not valuable. You should have never been born. Who do you think you are? You're a no good, worthless, piece o' trash."

Further continuing His discourse of love, Truth says to me, "Felicia, you're like a Rembrandt, a Monet, an original Van Goh, but you see yourself as a worthless copy." I love art. What Jesus said struck a chord with me. An original Rembrandt, Monet or Van Gogh painting would be procured for nothing less than thirty million dollars and some as much as eighty to ninety million dollars. That's a LOT of money. "You really see me like that?" I asked. "I see everyone like that," Jesus replied, "I have created each person to be a masterpiece, a display of My splendor. The evil one lies to the race of men and their eyes have become darkened to the truth of their worth. You are valuable. You are worthy. You are significant."

Feeling led to pick up the Bible, Truth led me to Jeremiah 1:5, *"Before I formed you in the womb, I knew you."* Shattering more of that stronghold, Truth reached deep into my wounded soul and began to apply healing. "Felicia, the truth is, you're no accident. I knew you before I ever placed you in your mom's womb. I decided the day and season into which you would be birthed. You have purpose. You have destiny. I meant for you to be on this earth. Even the betrayal, the rejection and the abandonment you've experienced will all be turned to good. I am so sorry you had to experience those things. That life was not my best for you, but I am One who can turn all things to good. Will you trust me? Even in this, will you trust me?"

With a resounding, "Yes, Lord, I'll trust you," the voice of the accuser began to quiet and more lies were replaced with truth. Healing love began to flow into wounded places. Even though I sat with Jesus as a married woman with a life and four kids, that little twelve year old girl who had given herself away in search of affirmation, affection and attention needed this truth spoken into the depths of her heart to heal her broken places and to see herself differently. I repented for seeing myself through the evil one's lens instead of living my life in agreement with how Father God sees me. I repented for not valuing the treasure of my virginity and giving away freely something I had deemed so cheaply. For the first time in my life, I realized I was meant to be born. Never again would I feel the sting of rejection when my momma would say the oft-repeated phrase, "You better be glad I didn't believe in abortion or you wouldn't be here." Jesus had taken the sting and the harm out of the phrase. It could no longer damage me because Love had restored that part of me to wholeness.

I allowed Holy Spirit to come and strip away every false label that had been stuck on me: "You're a whore. You're fast. You're easy. You're a cheap date. You're no good. You're invisible. You ain't worth shit. You're just like yo' momma. You're just like your daddy." Like Lazarus being unbound from his mummification, the dead was coming to life. Not only did He peel away the labels, Father God began to label me with His identification. "Felicia," He said, "I am the One who placed it in the heart of your family to name you that. You are joy. You are happy. You are strength. Strong warrior woman divine. I wove tenacity in you. You are my Beloved. You are my chosen one. How I delight in you."

And with every word, the affirmation, affection and attention my little twelve year old heart longed for was filled to overflowing with the Father's love. And that little girl ran into the arms of the Father I had been longing for. The One whose arms I could run into and would embrace me tightly. For I had never experienced the embrace of a father or heard the words I love you spoken by my own dad. I would exist some forty-one years on the earth before I ever heard my natural father say the words, "I love you" to me. But this day, Father's embrace and those very words would be etched upon my soul.

What about you? Have labels of false identity been attached to you that prevent you from seeing your worth? Do you see yourself as valuable?

Do you love yourself like you're worth eighty million dollars? If not, would you like to see yourself the way Father God sees you?

I invite you to pray this prayer with me: *Father, I haven't always believed the best about me. I repent for believing and agreeing with the lies of the evil one more than I have believed Your truth about me. I repent for living out of a false identity and labels that others have attached to my being. I repent for getting my significance from what others thought about me instead of what You think about me.*

Father God, what are the lies I've believed about my identity? What are the lies I've believed about my value? What are the lies I've believed about my self worth?

On a sheet of paper, or in your journal, write the word:

LIE:

Once you've written down every lie He shares with you, pray this prayer: *I renounce and break agreement with the lie that ... Holy Spirit, drain that lie out of me and every thing that came with it.*

Fill in the blank with the lies that He has revealed to you. Continue this prayer for each lie.

Holy Spirit, when was the first time I began to believe this lie?

Listen to what He says or shows you.

If He brings people to mind say: _____ *I forgive you for influencing me to believe that I was worthless, that I was not valuable. I forgive you for...* (Be specific about the things you need to forgive them for.)

Now, let's take a moment to hand Jesus every false label that's been stuck on you. First, let's ask Holy Spirit what the labels are. You can also list any that come to mind yourself, but it's imperative to invite the Spirit of Truth into this process.

Holy Spirit, what are the false labels that I need to remove from my identity?

Once Holy Spirit highlights these labels to you, hand them to Jesus.

Jesus, I hand you low self esteem, low self worth, self deprecation, (insert the labels He gave you). What would you like to give me in exchange?

Be sure to write down what He gave you.

Then ask Holy Spirit, What's the truth about my value?

Underneath the lie, write:

TRUTH:

List the truth that Holy Spirit gives you. As Holy Spirit reveals the truth to you, repeat them out loud welcoming that truth into every part of you.

I receive the truth that... into every part of me.

Finally, let's ask Father God for His intent for your identity.

Father God, how do you see me?

Father God, how do you want me to see myself?

CHAPTER 9

DEALING WITH DAD

Even as that thought, that my dad had never been able to say I love you to me or embrace me in the way that I needed to be loved, flitted across my mind, Holy Spirit was there to show me my dad, the hurting young man who graduated valedictorian of his class but left college after a few years and went to war in Vietnam. Holy Spirit showed me a glimpse of the pain he saw as a rifleman on the front line of the pesticide laden fields of Hanoi in that gruesome war and the sorrow he felt which he quickly drowned night after night in a fifth of liquor. I saw a young man forced to be a father out of honor as the consequence of a bad decision instead of choosing the role of husband and father born of love and devotion. I saw his struggles to be a good provider and to love his family as ill equipped as he was in doing so. I saw the man whose own father showed him no mercy and no love. I saw the man who experienced his own version of abuse and violence at the hands of an angry and alcoholic father. And again, I saw the effects of generational spirits influencing my family in rage and addictions. My heart broke for that young man who is my dad.

Seeing him as Father God sees him allowed me to forgive him and to release him from every expectation I had of what a father should be. And with that, I chose to let my father off the hook and to set him free from my IOUs. For the truth is Jesus had forgiven my dad of his sins just as he had forgiven me of mine. Both of our accounts had been settled by His death. Our slates wiped clean to begin anew. The truth I needed to come into agreement with was that my father owed me nothing. In releasing my dad and facing the emptiness of not being loved the way I needed or wanted to be loved, Father God gently spoke into my heart and said, "I'll be a Father to you." And true to His word, He has been a loving, gracious and very kind Father to me.

How about you? What has your experience with your father been? Has he been absent, angry, distant, abusive, uncaring, dispassionate, cold? Do you need to forgive your dad? Perhaps like my father, your father never learned how to express his emotions, verbalize his I love you's. Perhaps he failed to accurately re-present Father God to you.

Often we see Father God the same way we see our earthly fathers. I only knew anger in my home and rules in our church. I grew up never hearing my father say I love you or preachers say that there was a Father in Heaven who loved me. I wrongly assumed that God was angry because my parents were. I definitely was. Heck, almost everyone I knew was angry, bitter, harsh, mean and vindictive.

If you feel your father misrepresented God to you in any way or didn't love you the way you needed to be loved, I'd like to invite you to pray this prayer aloud:

Dad, I was hurt by your (anger, distance, lack of love, lack of attention, abuse, neglect, abandonment, rejection…you choose the words that most describe what you feel). *I forgive you for misrepresenting Father God to me. I forgive you for not loving me the way I needed to be loved. I forgive you for not taking the time to be there for me. I forgive you for not embracing me, for not speaking into my identity. I forgive you for not affirming me. I forgive you for not keeping me safe. Dad, I release you today. I release you from every expectation that I have of what a father should be or what a father should do. And in so doing, I take the hook out of my heart that binds me to your trespasses and I tear up every IOU that I am holding against you. Dad, you owe me nothing. You don't owe me an apology, an explanation, nothing. And I bless you, Dad, to be the man of God that He has created you to be. Father God, I repent for seeing You the way I've seen my earthly Father. Give me an accurate picture of who You are and who You want to be to me.*

Now let's ask Holy Spirit: *Holy Spirit, what lies have I believed to be true about my dad?*

Listen closely to what He says. If He reveals any lies to you, grab a pen so you can write them down. On a sheet of paper, write the word:

LIE:

Once you've written down every lie He shares with you, pray this prayer: *I renounce and break agreement with the lie that ...*

Fill in the blank with the lies that He has revealed to you. Continue this prayer for each lie.

Then ask Holy Spirit, *What's the truth about my dad?*

Underneath the lie, write:

TRUTH:

List the truth that Holy Spirit gives you.

Maybe you've read that and you can't relate. You have a good dad and a great relationship with him. That's beautiful! I so desire that to be my kid's testimony of their relationship with their dad as well. But, let's face it. No one is perfect. And oft times when we elevate people to pedestal worthy places in our hearts, we remove the need for Father God to fill us with His love since we obtain all we need from the people we've placed in those high places. Even those of us who grew up with good fathers and have enjoyed amazing relationships with them still need to know the love of Father God in a way that no human can satiate. So I encourage you to join the process at this point and complete the heart exercise with us. Perhaps there is something here Father would like to highlight to you as well.

Now, ask Holy Spirit these two questions and be sure to record your answers:

Holy Spirit, how do you see my father?

Holy Spirit, how do you want ME to see my father?

Finally, let's restore your image of Father God. He wants you to see Him as He is and to know His great love for you. So let's ask Him:

Father God, what lies have I believed about you?

Listen closely to what He says. If He reveals any lies to you, grab a pen so you can write them down. On a sheet of paper, or in your journal, write the word:

LIE:

Once you've written down every lie He shares with you, pray this prayer: *I renounce and break agreement with the lie that …*

Fill in the blank with the lies that He has revealed to you. Continue this prayer for each lie.

Then ask Him, *Father God, what's the truth about who You are?*

Underneath the lie, write:

TRUTH:

List the truth He shows you.

Let's end by asking God to give you a picture of how He wants you to see Him. Close your eyes, take a deep breath and ask the question:

Father God, how do you want me to see You?

Father God, how do you want me to see myself?

Be sure to record any mental images that popped into your mind's eye when you asked the question or any thoughts or impressions that came to mind.

Chapter 10

Facing Disappointment

I went through a series of quiet times in which I kept seeing an image of a woman speaking to crowds. Sometimes in the image she would be speaking to crowds of ten, other times, hundreds and at other times, what seemed like a massive amount of people. I remember marveling at the dress of the woman, and the confidence that exuded from her person. What struck me most was that the words from her mouth seem to pierce the hearts of her listeners like arrows hitting their mark.

Then one day on yet another encounter with Truth, I lay on my floor marinating in the melodious stream of instrumental worship music turning my heart and my affection towards Jesus. All of a sudden, I saw myself as a little girl at play dressed in the same clothes of the woman I had seen speaking to the various crowds. Her clothes lay hanging off my arms and the shoes four sizes too big and yet there I was playing alone dressed in this woman's clothes. In seconds, my heart connected with the truth the picture had been telling me for days and I gasped aloud. That woman was me! In the moment that truth pierced my heart, I heard Jesus say, "Felicia, will you look at me now?"

Even though Jesus and I were getting closer, there were still walls that prevented my heart from trusting. And here He was with the Spirit of Truth to peel away yet another layer of deception. You see, I believed the lie that I was a disappointment. I knew a lot of my choices had led my parents, grandparents, teachers and friends to be disappointed in me, but I had equated my doing to my being. And I believed the lie that Father God saw me as a disappointment and was as disappointed in me as others. I believed the lie that Father God would never accept me. I believed the lie that I wasn't good enough, couldn't do enough to please Him. I believed the lie that I was worthless and insignificant. And even though He had brought Truth to so many areas of my heart, I still kept Him at a distance because I believed the lie that His eyes only held sadness and disappointment towards me.

But in that moment of looking up, I caught a mere glimpse of Jesus' eyes and I knew the truth. Hebrews 12:3 says Jesus is the EXACT representation of the Father. And in Jesus' eyes, there was no disappointment. There was no sadness. His eyes were filled with so much love towards me that one glimpse caused me to be overwhelmed by His deep care and concern for me. In that moment, I knew I was loved. Not just that Jesus loved me, but loved by His Father as well.

I asked Jesus if it was okay to remove the wall that separated me from His Father. Immediately, in my mind's eye, I saw a picture of a little bitty dog standing guard of a partially torn down brick wall. Some places on the wall had been busted through as if smashed by a sledgehammer and other parts of the wall still had high places on it. The little dog looked something akin to a terrier and was barking so ferociously, foaming at the mouth as if he was rabid.

Jesus assured me I no longer had to rely on myself for protection. He said His Father would protect me and that He was so big I could live inside of Him. He asked me if this was what I wanted. I assented. With my yes, Holy Spirit slung the sledgehammer and the remaining bricks went scattering into smithereens.

There kneeling on the other side, arms outstretched was Father God. I ran into His embrace and He loved me. Father God picked me up, swung me around and laughed. His heart seemed to say, "Oh, how I've waited for this day! Longed for this day." His eyes were alight with merriment. I realized that Truth had visited me with a living revelation of the scripture, *"I am the way, the truth and the light, no one comes to the*

Father but by Me."[17] For indeed, Jesus had facilitated my homecoming into the Father's embrace. In my bedroom that day, I felt a warmth in the pit of my belly and every limb was weak as Father embraced me. I could feel myself begin to tingle from the top of my head as Love spread through me.

Father's great love for us compels us to agree with His blueprint of our original intent. The truth is God is a Master Builder and He uniquely and divinely designed each one of us before He ever placed us in our mother's womb. You cannot live in Love without thinking differently about God and about yourself. In fact, learning to live loved is learning to live in complete agreement with the you Father God intended you to be before the foundation of the world was laid. That's how long He's had you in mind.

Living inside the Father's love changed my life and the overflow of His love began to spill out of me into my relationship with my husband and children. A home that was once stifled under the whims of mom's present mood swing was released to flourish in an environment of love, joy, peace and grace. Everything about our lives became different in a better, more purposeful way.

Some time later, I penned an allegory entitled, 'Coming Out of the Closet', to capture the significance of awakening to my true self as revealed through Father's love. His loving embrace gave me the confidence and permission I needed to step into the me He had created me to be before the earth was laid and the world formed.

One day as I was communing with Him, I fell into a deep sleep with my face upon my pillow.

As I slept, He touched me and I saw myself hid in the furtherest recesses of my closet, cowering in the darkness; kneeling in the corner; arm above my head to protect myself from the world and all therein.

The closet door gently creaked open and I made not a sound, willing

---

17   John 14:6

myself invisible, afraid for what was next.

Immediately a fragrance overtook me, so sweet was the smell, I lowered my hand and lifted my head to draw in more of the sweet smelling savor.

Much to my dismay, I realized, I had been found out! My secret place uncovered! Exposed to the One.

But wait, what is that look in His eyes? They look like dove's eyes. So peaceful, so safe. "I wanna go with You," I thought. "Am I safe with you?"

As if He could read my thoughts, He smiled, extended His hand and bid me, "Come. Come up here. I went to prepare a place for you so that you could be with me where I am. My Dad has many rooms in His house. If that were not the truth, I wouldn't say it to you. I promised I wouldn't leave you as an orphan. I came for you. I promised I wouldn't leave you comfortless. Have you met Helper, My friend? Your friend? He will guide you into all truth. Why has your soul been so downcast? Put your hope in Me alone. Here, let me take this (False Security - my black cape). And here let me take this (Extra - my false comfort). And here, can I have that (Wall - my defense mechanism I've used all of my life to survive)? And if you'd like, you can hand me those lies, those fears, and that ball of unforgiveness. No pressure, only if you'd like. Come, come walk with me through the valley of the shadow of death. It's okay. Nothing to fear now, I am with you. My rod and My staff, they will provide comfort for you. And you can have as much of Me as you want for surely goodness and mercy are with you. Beloved, I have good and perfect gifts for you, compliments of My Father and Your Father. You see, you never sweep a house clean and leave it empty. So for everything you've given Me on our journey together, I want to restore to you gifts that were rightfully yours from the beginning: My signet ring, this is your all access pass to the Kingdom. All of heaven is open to you. There is nothing on hold from you. With My ring, you shall decree a thing and it shall be established for you and light will shine on your ways. I also bestow upon you, the robe of righteousness – no longer do you need to clean yourself, prove yourself. You are forever secure in My love. Every decision made from My love, every thought, every action, every word, every deed done from My love will be correct.

To live from My love is to have My mind. My scepter is always extended to you. The veil is torn in two. You can forever come and be with Me where I am. You never have to leave My presence. In me is fullness of joy and at My right hand, I always have pleasures. I have also for you a jeweled crown. I am your defender. My love is your greatest weapon. No longer are you to merely survive, I hereby crown you to thrive."

Though I was weak and faint, with every step, He lent me His strength. With every word spoken from His lips, I stood more erect. We walked and walked, hands intertwined, sometimes just walking and saying no words.

As I continued to sleep, I looked again and realized no longer was I a little scared abandoned orphan girl walking with Him. That person was no more. The pauper was made alive to God in Christ Jesus!

Awakened to her identity, now a radiant princess adorned in her royalty.

Who is that dancing upon the mountain? You are a radiant song, a breath of fresh air, still magnolias hung on its branches. Who is that partnering with heaven to release love on the earth? You are My fair one, My beloved, My bride. Who is that? Who are you?

I am the called out one. You have called me out of darkness, out of the recesses of my closet corner into Your marvelous light. Good-bye false security, good-bye wall, good-bye lies. Good-bye false comfort. Hello Father and all you offer.

'Tis true that when your eye is clear your whole body is full of light.[18] For after that baptism of love, everything became more clear and vibrant. When you have a revelation of how big God is and just how much He loves you, you'll soon discover that that love compels you to allow Jesus to radiate through you.

What about you? Have you lived with the nagging sense that you have disappointed God with your choices or your lifestyle? Perhaps

---

18 Matthew 6:22

people have even, in the past, labeled you a disappointment. Do you find that you keep parts of yourself walled off from others? Perhaps you're afraid of being hurt again; maybe the risk feels too great to take. I invite you to pray with me.

Father God, I repent for seeing You the way I have seen others. I repent for believing and agreeing with the lie that You are disappointed in me. I repent for not believing the truth about who You are and how You see me. Jesus, I hand You disappointment. I hand You disillusionment. What would You like to give me in exchange?

Be sure to write down what He gives you.

Holy Spirit, when was the first time I believed the lie that Father God was disappointed in me?

LIE:

Once you've written down every lie He shares with you, pray this prayer: I renounce and break agreement with the lie that ...

Fill in the blank with the lies that He has revealed to you. Continue this prayer for each lie.

Holy Spirit, what's the truth?

TRUTH:

List the truth He shows you.

Father God, I repent for not trusting You enough to protect me. I repent for feeling like I needed to protect myself. Holy Spirit, when was the first time I believed the lie that I needed to protect myself?

Listen to what Holy Spirit shows you. If there is someone you need to forgive for making you feel like you needed to protect yourself, go ahead and do that now. I encourage you to also forgive your earthly father, as it is the role of our dads to protect us and take care of us. When we take on self-protection as a defense mechanism, it is a clear indicator that we did not receive the protection we needed from our fathers or that we have rejected the protection they've offered.

Dad, I forgive you for not being there to protect me the way I needed to be protected. I forgive you for leaving me exposed and vulnerable. Jesus, I sever my agreement with self-protection and I nail it to the cross of Jesus. Jesus, what would you like to give me in exchange for self-protection?

Be sure to record what He gives you.

What about Father God? How is your relationship with Him? Do you see Him as a Father who loves you? A Father who embraces you? A Father who cheers you on and is there for you? Are you presently experiencing Him loving you? Listen with your spirit to the truth about who Father God is to you.

Zep. 3:17 "The LORD your God is in your midst, A victorious warrior. He will exult over you with joy, He will be quiet in His love, He will rejoice over you with shouts of joy."

2 Cor. 6:18 "And I will be a father to you, And you shall be sons and daughters to Me," Says the Lord Almighty."

Gal. 4:6-7 "Because you are sons, God has sent forth the Spirit of His Son into our hearts, crying, "Abba! Father! Therefore you are no longer a slave, but a son; and if a son, then an heir through God."

John 16:27 "for the Father Himself loves you, because you have loved Me and have believed that I came forth from the Father."

Can you see Father God loving you in that manner? If not, let's ask Holy Spirit what is preventing you from receiving Father's embrace.

Holy Spirit, is there a wall separating me from Father God?

If He says yes, ask Him to show you the wall.

Holy Spirit, what does this wall look like?

Some of you may see an actual picture or snapshot like I did with the torn down bricks and the dog. Some of you might see or hear a word or experience a feeling or an emotion. Be sure to record what you are seeing, hearing, sensing or feeling. After you have done that, pray this prayer with me:

Holy Spirit, is it safe for my wall to come down?

If He says yes, then continue with this prayer: *Holy Spirit, I give you permission to come and tear this wall down.*

Once you sense the wall that separates you from Father God has been removed, ask Jesus to take you to the Father.

Jesus, would you take me to Your Father and My Father?

Once you are with Father God, ask Him the following questions:

Father God, whom have you created me to be? Father God, how do you see me? How would you like me to see myself? What lies am I believing that are preventing me from seeing myself the way You see me?

LIE:

Once you've written down every lie He shares with you, pray this prayer: *I renounce and break agreement with the lie that ...*

Fill in the blank with the lies that He has revealed to you. Continue this prayer for each lie.

Holy Spirit, what's the truth?

TRUTH:

List the truth He shows you.

CHAPTER 11

THE SEARCH FOR SIGNIFICANCE

That specific encounter with Truth changed a lot for me. It was as if His eyes became a mirror and when I looked at Him, I saw myself. And it seems that overnight, I was completely transformed into this new, confident, secure, loving, powerful and free person.

I had seen this picture of greatness in Jesus' eyes and it captivated me. Me speaking to crowds of ten, hundreds, the masses, sharing relevant messages on the finished work, preaching about grace and bringing a revelation of the Father's love. Mentoring. Equipping. Empowering. Raising up leaders and world changers. Giving my life to see people get it. Teaching others how to live in constancy. Bringing believers into agreement with God so they could learn to live as sons and daughters in right relationship with Father God empowered by the Holy Spirit.

This became the desire that burned within me. This became my sweet spot. I gave up a decade long career with a direct sales company that I absolutely loved just so I could pursue this lofty call. Everything in me was shouting, "For this cause was I born. For this cause have I come into the world!"

Sounds noble, doesn't it? Why yes, yes it does, such a grand and lofty thing to accomplish for the Lord. And yet, as I encountered Truth yet again, He showed me that even this, as noble and honorable as it is, it is all dung when held up beside Father God's picture of greatness.

Truth asked the hard questions of me: If there was never another pulpit would I still be significant? If there was never another applause would I still be significant? If every atta boy faded away, would I still be significant? If I never taught again, preached again, would I still be significant?

The answer Truth shouted was a resounding YES! "Felicia," Truth said, "your significance is not tied to what you do. Your significance isn't found in you being a world changer or a history maker. Your significance isn't attached to the end of a microphone or how many speaking engagements you have penned on your calendar. You are significant because You are mine. Even if you never do another thing for Me, I alone am enough for you. And you for Me. If you sit all day on your couch in your pajamas communing with Me, being with Me, receiving My love into every part of you, you are great. Even in the mundane, routine monotony of everyday life, you are significant. When all is stripped away, you remain significant."

Sitting with Truth, I realized that I was seeing greatness in light of what I did. An easy mistake that fuels discontent and breeds ambition. Father God sees greatness in light of who I am. A right belief that breeds confidence and security. I'm great because I am born of God. Acts 17:28 says, *"we are His offspring."* I am great because I have been re-presented to my Heavenly Father as a full grown son (daughter) having received the spirit of adoption whereby I cry, "Abba, Father" or "Daddy, Daddy!" I'm great because I've chosen the good part, which is living life fully loved. I am great because I choose to live as a son (daughter), in the grace of today, abiding, communing, partnering with Him as I speak what He says and do what He does, loving the one that is right in front of me. This is the height to which He has called me.

When I understood Daddy God's picture of greatness, it eliminated my need for striving. I no longer find myself trying to achieve some far off status. Because of what Jesus has done, I already am. I am confident that Daddy God is good and He is for me. I get to be great in every situation or circumstance because I am hid in His bigness and His goodness for me. I don't need a stage to be great. I am great in my living room. I am great in my pajamas. I am great at a lunch counter. I'm great in the park or wherever life takes me. Greatness doesn't come in an event. It comes in the revelation that I am a son or I am a daughter and because my Daddy God is great, I am called to be as He is.

Greatness looks like peace – the exemption from rage and havoc of war. I am great because in my Dad I get a free pass from madness, from violence, from uncontrollable anger. I get a free pass from destruction and chaos. Not that life is absent of those things, however those things no longer happen to me. My heart, my soul and spirit are not ravaged by destruction or chaos anymore. I am great when I am completely at peace with myself, with Abba, and with my present life. I am great when I am my same self no matter the situation or circumstance. I am great when I am living in Father's security, which frees me from danger. I am great when I am living in Father's safety, which frees me from loss. I am great when I am living in Father's prosperity, which frees me to live a life that is successful, flourishing, and thriving. I am great when I am living in Father's joy, which frees me to experience felicity or happiness.

All this time, I was focusing on an external picture of greatness. When Truth came, He showed me that Papa God was focusing on an internal picture. I was trying to do to be. Papa God simply called me to be. And from my being, I do. My internal reality creates my external reality.

I was asking Father God, "how can I serve you today? What can I do for you today, Lord?" And He would say with such grace, "Come sit with me. Come be with me. Come play with me. Come sing with me. Come fly with me." Always fun. Always free. Always relational. Always my choice. Often times never saying a word, just sitting…being. I wanted to change the world. He wanted to change me. I had articulated my purpose in life. I had a mission and so did He. His yoke is easy and His burden is light.

Somewhere along the way, I believed the lie that if I wasn't doing something big for God, I wasn't being great. I believed the lie that I needed to be a part of something bigger than myself to be a world changer. Truth spoke into the depth of my heart, "Felicia, the biggest thing you can be a part of is your union with Me and I accomplished that for you through My death, burial and resurrection. If you never do another single exploit in the name of God, it won't discount your greatness any less or esteem your significance any more. You simply learning to live as my daughter is the greatest thing you could ever do." As Truth spoke, I realized that to master the fullness of living life fully loved is to live a life of peace, safety, security, acceptance, rest, and trust. It is total confidence and reliance on God as my Father. It is a life hid in Christ who is our life.[19]

This is why Truth came. I am because He is. If I never do another thing, Papa God, Jesus and Holy Spirit, He alone is enough for me. In Him, I am found. In Him, I am free. When I understand fully in my inner being that my greatness, my significance is tied to my sonship, no matter what task or role I find myself in: speaking to thousands or cleaning toilets, I can live head high and heart abandoned to the One.

When I have peace, I am living in greatness. When I have safety, security, prosperity, trust, acceptance, I am living in greatness. When I'm confident in Daddy God's bigness and His goodness for me, I am living in greatness. Every day I wake up and I feel the Father loving me, I am living in my sweet spot. It's the greatest moment of my life to live life fully loved.

Right perspective changes everything.

What about you? Are you living in greatness? Has the issue of significance been settled in your heart? Or do you find yourself striving, living a life devoid of peace?

If so, I invite you to pray this prayer with me: *Father God, I repent for striving. I repent for equating my significance to my doing instead of my being. Holy Spirit, I invite you to give me a right perspective of what my greatness looks like through the eyes of Father God.*

---

19 Col. 3:4

Father God, what does greatness in You look like?

Be sure to write it down.

Holy Spirit, what lies have I believed about my significance?

Holy Spirit, what lies have I believed that has prevented me from walking in peace?

Be sure to record any lies He reveals to you. Then pray: *I renounce and break agreement with the lie that...*

Holy Spirit, what's Your truth?

Write down the truth He gives you.

Now pray: *I receive Your truth into every part of me.*

CHAPTER 12

RECEIVING COMFORT

I remember one night shortly after Doug and I met, I was lying in his bed asleep with one foot dangling out of the bed. He awoke early the next morning for physical training with his Naval Reserve Officers Training Corp and noticed how I was sleeping. When he returned from PT, he inquired about my sleeping position and I told him I slept like that in case I needed to run. With a puzzled look on his face, he asked, "Who hurt you that bad that you're afraid to get all the way in the bed?" I responded, "No one in particular. I just don't trust people." He accepted my answer but I could tell it left more questions in his head than he started with.

Like an animal that's been wounded, I cowered inside at the first sign of trouble. Outwardly, I lived in a fight or flight stance. There wasn't one person in my life I trusted. I remember when I finally accepted the truth that I was pregnant. I went to visit my favorite aunt and confided in her that I was pregnant. I was sixteen, lost and confused. I was longing for comfort, looking for counsel. If anyone could provide that for me, I just knew it would be her. When I divulged my secret, instead of comfort, she remarked with disdain, "Oh, so you think you're grown now, uh?" Her words felt like a slap in the face and I didn't know what to do with them. I swallowed, changed the subject and with as much dignity as I could muster, left her home as fast as my two legs would carry me out of there.

That experience shattered the last vestige of trust I had in people. Naturally, it would be these two memories in which Truth would visit me to heal the wounds created by broken trust.

Danny Silk in his book, *Keep Your Love On* (Silk, Keep Your Love On, 2013) has a chart that shows a trust cycle and a mistrust cycle. And in it, he says, "Trust is developed when there is a need. I express my need. There is a response to my need. The need is satisfied and I am comforted." The converse of that is true as well, "Mistrust happens when there is a need. The need is expressed. There is no response to my need. The need is left unmet and no comfort is experienced."

On this particular day, quiet instrumental worship music playing softly in the background, I laid down on my bedroom floor. As Jesus joined me there, He lay beside me and reached to take my hand. Fingers intertwined with His, my world became black. I literally felt as if I was suffocating. Fear gripped me as claustrophobia overtook me and I began to panic. I opened my eyes and began to gasp for breath. Lifting my head off the floor to confirm that I was indeed alone, I began to look around the room. Tuning into Jesus I asked, "What in the WORLD was that?!" To which He replied, "You know that I love you. Do you not?" "Yes, Lord, I know," I responded. "Can you trust that I'll be with you no matter where we go?" As His peace strengthened me, I replied with courage, "Yes."

In my spirit, I felt prompted to lie back down on the floor. So I did. Closing my eyes and tuning in to the spontaneous flow of the Holy Spirit, I again felt overcome with blackness and fear. Mustering up courage, I asked Jesus, "Where are we?" "In your mother's womb," He replied. "Why am I afraid?" I asked. He said, "you drank in your mother's fear when you were in the womb. It was passed on to you through the bloodline. Since you were conceived, you have had needs. Some were met. Some were not. The evil one has deceived you to focus primarily on your unmet needs and it has severed your ability to trust."

"Lord, I do trust you," I replied. "Felicia," He said, "you have an image of trust but Father wants to give you the confidence of security." Holy

Spirit asked, "What do you feel?" "I feel afraid, alone, scared." "Where is Jesus?" He asked. Peering into the darkness, I searched for Jesus.

I literally started experiencing flickers of light dancing underneath my eyelids. And I felt the darkness shift to a white light. As the light began to radiate within me, I heard the Spirit of Truth begin to speak, "Felicia, you have often felt invisible, forgotten, passed over. You have often felt as if your voice didn't matter and that your cries went unheard. Your tears wasted.

My child, today, I speak truth to the babe in her mother's womb. As one whom his mother comforts so I will comfort you and you will be comforted. I brought you safely out of your mother's womb and I made you to trust me. The provision for every need was there before you could even express your need. My answer to you has never changed. Indeed, my yes is yes and it remains so over your life." Again, I felt Father's liquid love being poured into all of me. As that was happening, I heard Father God, say, "My child, I am big enough and kind enough to fulfill your every need. Daughter, I am for you. My child, receive My comfort today."

Years later, I would find myself on a prayer retreat in Moravian Falls, NC. As my friends and I gathered to pray on prayer mountain, we sat on a huge rock that overlooked thousands of trees. A wide open expanse separated us from the trees. Gazing into the distance, all of a sudden I saw trees become golden yellow like wheat basking in a bright sun and Father God filled that empty expanse with Himself. He was so so tall, thousands of feet high it seemed. Literally, His legs came up to where we were and his torso extended beyond that. The span of His arms outstretched filled the width of the expanse and suddenly no part of that space was void or empty. That revelation of how BIG God is has boosted my confidence in God as my Father. Truly, I am just a little bitty daughter with a great big Dad. I know He has my back. I know His love for me is even deeper and wider than the expanse He filled with Himself that day. In His love, I have found that I can be confidently secure in Him. There's no doubt in my mind that He is who He says He is or that He will do or be what He says He will do or be. No one can convince me otherwise.

Because He has met my expressed needs more times that I can count in more ways than I could have ever imagined, I truly trust Him. I have a joyful anticipation that good is always coming to me because that's what Father promises me. Even bigger than Him meeting my needs, as important as that is, as I've deepened my relationship with Him and gotten to know Him, I know His character is unfailing, His nature consistent. He can only be who He says He is. He can only do what He says He will do. And I know without a shadow of a doubt that He is for me. As I have spent time with Him, I find myself more and more allowing His Son to freely live through me.

1 John 4:16-17 We have come to know and have believed the love which God has for us. God is love, and the one who abides in love abides in God, and God abides in him. By this, love is perfected with us, so that we may have confidence in the day of judgment; because as He is, so also are we in this world.

What about you? Do you trust in who God is? Or do you trust in what He does?

What I discovered as the Spirit of Truth taught me is that if I only trust in what God does, when He doesn't do what I think He should do or when what I want Him to do in the time I want Him to do it in doesn't happen as I think it should, then I can easily become offended at God. Mistrust. Doubt. Unbelief. Hopelessness. As a result of me blaming God for not coming through for me, all of these become attributes of my thought life and characteristics that I wrongly assign to His nature. Putting my trust in what God can do for me or what I want Him to do for me leads to opportunities to build a case against God.

Trusting in who He is only strengthens the bonds of our connection and deepens my love for Him. He is kind. He is faithful. He is good. He is love. He is all knowing, always there, consistent. In every situation, I can always count on Him to be who He is. Because I know that to be true of His nature, I can trust who He wants to be to me. He withholds no good thing.

In Him, my identity has been transformed. That day in Moravian Falls, NC, for me, the issue of protection was forever settled. Whenever there is even a tiny inkling to retreat within myself and grab self-protection, I only have to remember Father God filling the expanse with Himself. Immediately, my perspective shifts, my heart warms and I say aloud, "Thank you Papa that I'm your little girl. Big, big God. Little bitty devil."

The more we trust God, the freer we are regardless of circumstances. Deep, intimate relationships can only be built on foundations of trust.

Trust happens when you allow me to see inside of you so that I might get to know the real you. What Jesus showed me in my truth encounter was that I had closed myself off to people. Actually, it had been an assignment of the evil one against me before I was ever birthed in the world. Through generational spirits that influenced my own sins, and through my own choosing, I had partnered with this evil assignment. From one bad, detrimental relationship to the next, the cards were stacked against me encouraging me to hide, to wall myself off, to keep others from knowing the real me out of fear of more rejection, further abandonment and betrayal. My heart had never been handled with care. It had been taken out of my chest, trampled on and pulverized, repeatedly.

Trust develops between two people when you handle each other's heart with care as you open up and show each other what's inside. Trust happens in relationships when truth is exchanged and there remains freedom and permission for each party to be who they are without being forced to conform or lose themselves in the relationship.

What about you? Are there things in your past that have prevented you from trusting other people? Prevented you from trusting God? Let's invite the Spirit of Truth to join us.

Holy Spirit, are there people I don't trust? If He says yes, ask Him, *whom do I need to forgive for influencing me to partner with mistrust and suspicion of people?*

As He brings these people to mind, walk through forgiveness using the prayer model we used for forgiving our mother and our father.

Holy Spirit, are there lies I'm believing that prevent me from trusting Father God?

Be sure to record any lies He reveals to you.

Holy Spirit, what's Your truth?

Write down the truth He gives you.

Holy Spirit, what are the areas of my life that need to be comforted?

When Holy Spirit begins to show you these areas, write them down on a piece of paper that you can later discard. As He brings these areas to mind, take note of any people that you need to forgive. Also take note of how each situation made you feel. Once you have this information, invite Holy Spirit, your Comforter to join you. Start with forgiving the person(s) who harmed or wronged you. Release and bless them. After you have done this, I invite you to pray this with me:

Holy Spirit, I ask that You come in the fullness of who You are. Would You edit out the pain and the trauma of this offense from my heart, my spirit, my soul and my thought life? Would You comfort me with Your love and Your peace and show me the truth You want me to believe about this person(s) and this situation?

Holy Spirit, what does it look like for me to receive Your comfort into every part of me?

Be sure to record what He says in a place that you can refer back to later on.

Holy Spirit, what would You like to do with my unmet needs?

Write down what He says. Then continue your prayer:

Jesus, I hand You every unmet need. I hand You every hole, every void, every longing, every desire that I have that has yet to be fulfilled. What would You like to give me in exchange?

Holy Spirit, what lies have I believed about these unmet needs?

Holy Spirit, what's the truth?

Holy Spirit, have I been influenced by the generational spirit of fear?

If He says yes, let's sever that spirit from having any more influence in your life.

Father God, I repent for my sins and my ancestor sins in partnering with the spirit of fear whether knowingly or unknowingly. I break all agreements with the spirit of fear that have existed in my family line, all generations back and all generations forward. And I sever my agreement with fear. Fear, I nail you and everything that came with you to the cross of Jesus. Jesus, what would you like to give me in exchange for fear? I bless my family line, all generations back and all generations forward with (insert here whatever it is Jesus gave you in exchange for fear).

Finally, let's pray this prayer to clear up any misconceptions of how we have seen Father God based on our issues with trust.

Father God, I repent for seeing You through the lens of doubt, mistrust, and unbelief. I repent for seeing You the way I've seen other people and their failures or mistakes. Father God, would You take everything I believe to be true about You, Jesus and Holy Spirit and sift it through Your love and Your perspective? Father God, I give You permission to purify my understanding of who You are. Father God, how do You want me to see You?

Be sure to record what He shows you.

CHAPTER 13

DEALING WITH SHAME

Finally, a day came when Truth and I were sitting together enjoying the quiet of each other's hearts and Jesus said to me, "Felicia, you know that time when you were sixteen?" I guess I'd hoped we could skip this time. But I had given Holy Spirit permission to weed the garden of my heart and to replace deception with truth. True to His nature, He had been a Comfort in the process and I was beginning to like this God whom I was finding to be so unlike the one I had, at the age of nine, only agreed to serve because I didn't want to go to hell.

Even though things were changing in our relationship and I was seeing Him differently, I still believed the lie that I had been branded irrevocably with that K and thus eternally damned. Yes, I know Jesus forgives our sins. But the red duct tape Christians wear on their mouths to protest those who have made the unfortunate decision of terminating a life led me to believe that in this one area, I was destined to be condemned forever. Their red covered mouths were a mockery to my forgiveness. The thump thump thump of that ultrasound machine from that wood paneled wall collided in the ears of my heart with such ferocity each time my eyes beheld these Christians.

I'd never looked at someone wearing red duct tape over their mouth and experienced a feeling of mercy, forgiveness or even conviction. The words LIFE so poignantly printed in capital letters across their lips seem to cry out with the blood of slain babies covering the moms of those babies with the shame of their decision and the condemning weight of their horrific act. As they cried out for justice for the lives of those slain babies, my heart would cry, where is the mercy for the one who committed that sin? I have never found it in the eyes of those whose mouths are taped in red. But, on this day, I found said mercy in the eyes of the One who is merciful.

As Jesus spoke to my heart, everything within me was glued to the ground. I couldn't bear to look up at Him and see pain in His eyes. It would have felt like rejection and that would have crushed me to the core of my being. The accuser of the brethren even then whispered lies against my Jesus, "you're gonna get it now." He laughed and mocked. But Jesus in His great love and kindness and persistence in bringing truth continued, "Felicia, you know that day when you went to the abortion clinic?" My heart nodded yes. "Did you know I was with you that day too?" Jesus inquired. "No," I admitted quite honestly, "I have never felt more alone in all of my life than I did on that day."

Instantly, I saw a picture of Jesus on the cross experiencing His darkest day on earth crying out to His Father, "My God, My God, why hast thou forsaken me?"[20] In that moment, I wondered truly did Father God, the God who said in Deuteronomy 31:6, Joshua 1:5 and Hebrews 13:5 that He would never leave us or forsake us, did that Father really abandon Jesus? Or did Jesus, like me in my darkest hour when I felt so all alone and abandoned, just feel like His Father had left Him? Could those sins heaped upon Jesus cause Him in that moment to feel like He had been abandoned?

As quickly as I saw that picture, I had a memory of that day. Jesus with me in the car, weeping as I sat silently weeping, He was interceding for me. Jesus walking with me down those steps into the clinic. Jesus sitting beside me on one of the hard black plastic chairs interceding for me as I read that pamphlet. Jesus with me in the dim room softening the heart of that counselor who looked on me with ridicule and derision. As I lay on the table, Jesus was looking at the monitor with love as the

---

20   Psalm 22:1

life of the little baby growing inside of me was so vividly portrayed, stroking my hair, hand on my shoulder releasing His peace into me. Jesus with me in the booth at Pizza Hut, walking with me through the mall as we passed the time away. Jesus entering the clinic with me once again and walking with me down the hall. "Even if you make your bed in Sheol, I am there."[21] Jesus standing by the doctor. Jesus taking the spirit of my little one even as the mass that was my baby was suctioned through the tube into that steel canister. Jesus ever present, grieving, weeping, releasing His peace.

And the broken fragmented pieces of my heart began to be cemented back together by the fact that even in my darkest hour, my stupidest choice, my worst mistakes, He never left me or abandoned me. There is One that has always been true to me. Even when I gave Him every reason to reject me, He never did. Oh the vastness of His great love for me. In the face of a love so great, so strong and so true, how could I not love Him back? How could I not think differently about Him and about myself?

When my mother and my father forsake me, then the Lord will take me up.[22] I'd finally come face to face with someone who wasn't afraid of my sin. He didn't run from me or try to control me or "make" me do the right thing. He was there all along and even when I chose badly, He still loved me. Who loves like that?

I looked Him in the face and knew with everything in me that I wanted to be transformed into His image and His likeness. I wanted to be a mom who could love like that, a friend, a wife who would love like that. What I did broke His heart. There's no confusion about that. His grieving and His weeping even as He interceded for me convinced me of that and yet, as He took me into this memory, there was no condemnation. There was no shame. There was no guilt. His mercy prevailed. His love, even on my worse day, covered a multitude of sin.

Then Jesus showed me a most glorious thing. The verse from 2

---

21 Psalm 139:8
22 Psalm 27:10

Corinthians 5:19 flashed before me, "that God was in Christ reconciling the world to Himself, not counting their trespasses against them, and He has committed to us the word of reconciliation," settling the question of where Father God was when Jesus was on the cross. As quickly as I saw that, I saw the K the evil one had tacked to my chest that I thought was my sentence of eternal damnation. Next, Jesus showed me a picture of me lying on the examination table being branded by the evil one with this false identity and then He showed me a picture of Him on the cross with Father God in Him and there emblazoned on His bruised and beaten body was my K all aflame. "See there, Felicia," Jesus quietly said, "an abortion is something you had, but Baby Killer is not who you are. I died even for that. The truth is I died not just for your K, but also for every person who has ever committed the sin of abortion. You are free from the guilt, shame and condemnation of that sin. Eternal damnation is not your inheritance. Eternal life is. No longer do you have to live under the weight of what you did because I died for that burden. You don't have to carry it. My yoke is a lot easier and my burden much lighter. I'm happy to exchange that with you, if you'd like." And so I reached up to my heart and I symbolically pulled out the nails that had held that K in place, stripped away the letter and handed it to Jesus. I'd never felt freer or lighter than I did in that moment!

And still there is more. Receiving the forgiveness offered to me by Jesus on that day in my bedroom and removing the labels of false identity that had led me to cower away in shame set the stage for a massive explosion of freedom in my life.

What about you? Is there some vestige of your worse mistake, your stupidest choice hanging over you causing you to cower in shame, guilt and condemnation?

When we connect our sin (past or present) to our identity, we invite shame. Shame keeps us hiding and invites fear and control to live in our hearts. Shame is a cloak that covers the real you. It keeps you from being who you really are. When we are ashamed, we tend to hide our real selves from others out of fear that others will discover the "dirty secrets" of our past. Jesus knows all about your past. And the truth about your past that He so desires you to grab a hold of is that He removed your shame and bought your past when He died on the cross. Your past is no longer rightfully yours. You don't have to continue living in the torment of past decisions. He came that you might have life, not shame.

Authenticity destroys shame. You have full permission from Father to be who He created you to be. Hand Jesus your cloak of shame and receive His robe of righteousness.

Let's see what Father would like to give you in place of shame. I invite you to pray with me: *Jesus, I repent for partnering with shame. I repent for taking on shame as a false identity and hiding the best of me from myself, from You, and from others. I repent for allowing the fear of past failures, bad choices and stupid mistakes to heap guilt and condemnation upon my soul. I repent for not receiving and believing in the fullness of what You did for me on the cross. I sever my agreement with shame and everything that came with it. Shame, Guilt, Condemnation, I nail you to the cross of Jesus. Jesus, what would You like to give me in exchange for shame, guilt and condemnation?*

Be sure to write down what He gives you.

Holy Spirit, what lies have I have believed that's kept me covered in shame?

Holy Spirit, what lies am I believing that is causing me to feel guilty and condemned?

Listen closely to what He says. If He reveals any lies to you, grab a pen so you can write them down. On a sheet of paper, or in your journal, write the word:

LIE:

Once you've written down every lie He shares with you, pray this prayer: *I renounce and break agreement with the lie that...*

Fill in the blank with the lies that He has revealed to you. Continue this prayer for each lie.

Holy Spirit, what's the truth?

TRUTH:

List the truth He shows you.

Jesus, when was the first time I partnered with shame?

Holy Spirit, is there anyone I need to forgive for influencing me to partner with shame?

Finally, let's end by asking God to give you a picture of His divine exchange. Close your eyes, take a deep breath and ask the question:

Father God, what does it look like for me to live free of shame?

Be sure to record any mental images that popped into your mind's eye when you asked the question or any thoughts or impressions that came to mind.

CHAPTER 14

FORGIVING FROM THE HEART

Encountering Truth once more on this same day, Jesus asked me if I was ready to forgive Bo Carter and Sabrina. "I've already forgiven them," I responded. "Felicia," He softly encouraged, "I want you to forgive them from your heart. Come, allow me to show you something." Immediately, I had an impression to read Matthew 18:21-35.

Then Peter came and said to Him, "Lord, how often shall my brother sin against me and I forgive him? Up to seven times? Jesus said to him, "I do not say to you, up to seven times, but up to seventy times seven. For this reason the kingdom of heaven may be compared to a king who wished to settle accounts with his slaves. When he had begun to settle them, one who owed him ten thousand talents was brought to him. But since did not have the means to repay, his lord commanded him to be sold, along with his wife and children and all that he had, and repayment to be made. So the slave fell to the ground and prostrated himself before him, saying, 'Have patience with me and I will repay you everything.' And the lord of that slave felt compassion and released him and forgave him the debt. But that slave went out and found one of his fellow slaves who owed him a hundred denarii; and he seized him and began to choke him, saying, 'Pay back what you owe. So his fellow slave fell to the ground and began to plead with him, saying, 'Have patience with me and I will repay you.' But he was unwilling and went and threw him in prison until he should pay back what was owed. So when his fellow slaves saw what had happened, they were deeply grieved and came and reported to their lord all that had happened. Then summoning him, his lord said to him, 'You wicked slave, I forgave you all that debt because you pleaded with me. 'Should you not also have had mercy on your fellow slave, in the same way that I had mercy on you?' And his lord, moved with anger, handed him over to the torturers until he should repay all that was owed him. My heavenly Father will also do the same to you, if each of you does not forgive his brother from your heart."

After reading this passage, I felt compelled to look up the word torment in my Strong's concordance. I found that it means grievous pain; to vex; to harass. In short, to torment means to experience the most amount of pain for the longest amount of time without killing someone. When you think about it that sounds a lot like hell or at least the version of hell that's been preached to me most of my life. As I reflected on that thought, I heard a Voice say, "You can have mercy or you can have judgment, but you can't have both. If you want mercy, you must extend mercy to those who have wronged you. If you want judgment, you will remain in torment." Forgiveness would cost me but unforgiveness would kill me.

Jesus preached this parable to those who were under the law. As such, many have interpreted forgiveness as something we have to do. If we don't, God won't forgive us. Through the finished work of the cross, we know that is the furtherest thing from the truth. On the cross, Jesus has already forgiven everyone for every sin ever committed. He's not going to get back on the cross and take that forgiveness back if we choose not to forgive. When Jesus forgave us on the cross, He gave us an unconditional gift. And He is not going to punish you by causing you to be tormented if you don't forgive. Unforgiveness and the negative emotions that accompany it is torment enough. Let me be completely clear, the torment that comes into a person's life as a result of unforgiveness is the consequence of our choice, NOT a punishment from God.

What truth knew about me was that I had forgiven Bo and Sabrina because I thought I had to, not because I wanted to and certainly not because my heart was in it. I was choosing forgiveness from a justice standpoint that if I didn't forgive them, God wouldn't forgive me. When Truth came to me, He was asking me to forgive from the heart, to give Bo and Sabrina the unconditional gift of forgiveness. Not because they deserved it, not because I would be forever tormented if I didn't but simply because I am made in His image and His likeness. He who had taken my heart of stone and given me a heart of flesh, was asking me to be in this world as He is and to extend to my perpetrators the gift of unconditional forgiveness because I had a heart to forgive.

To forgive, I had to be honest about each incident that happened to me; how it made me feel, how I responded to it, what lies I believed as a result of the incident and what behavior I portrayed because of the wounding that occurred. This is what I mean by "counting the cost." It wasn't pretty to face each offense and not shrink back. It was as if I was carted back to high school and reliving those days and weeks of seeing Bo Carter and Sabrina together. When the pain of a memory is as fresh as it was the day you experienced it, you are living in bitterness. And even though decades had past since my high school days, the bitterness that formed as a result of betrayal had never left me.

Bitterness was still demanding payment for those past wounds and offenses. This is what Jesus wanted me to see for He knew that in the day I truly forgave Bo Carter and Sabrina from my heart, the torment would cease. In Truth's great love for me, He showed me that the very people I had been judging and wanting to see get what they deserved owed me nothing. They had already received what they deserved. They had received from Father God mercy just as I had received mercy. James 2:13 says, *"Mercy triumphs judgment."* And so I forgave them, from the heart. I let the guilty go free.

Something incredible happened! I began to experience peace like I'd never felt before. I found myself genuinely happy. I found myself laughing and smiling. I found myself falling in love with Jesus. My home became full of joy and merriment. I found that in forgiving others, my heart began to sing. I was experiencing new levels of freedom. I began to love myself. I was able to love my kids, love others; genuinely love people. For the first time, my emotions were alive and present. I was becoming acquainted with joy and peace and it felt great.

Honestly, for a long time I never gave any more thought to this truth encounter. Then one day, I was driving down Interstate 264 headed towards our church and I passed a red Saab. Looking at the car, I thought, "Oh man, what a nice car. I kind of like that car," and continued on towards the off ramp. As I was exiting, joy welled up within me and I started laughing and clapping! I'm sure I looked crazy to the oncoming traffic, merging, smiling, laughing and clapping with no one else in the car besides myself. You see, that day so long ago when Bo Carter chose Sabrina over me, that afternoon when we went to the student parking lot to leave school, I watched Bo Carter get into Sabrina's tan Saab and drive off with her. Later, Bo Carter would finally get his own car. His car was a burgundy Saab that was an exact replica of Sabrina's car. From that point on, I hated Saab's with a passion. Literally, whenever I saw one on the interstate, I would cringe and get mad all over again. I would feel the rage from my intense hatred of those two and want to do bodily harm all over again. Saabs were like a trigger point for destructive negative emotions within me.

Seeing that Saab that day was the first external sign of the inner work that Father had begun to do on my heart! Some thirteen years later, I would actually run into Bo Carter. I was visiting Dawsonville. My parents had just bought a home and I was painting the interior walls of the bedrooms for them. I had ran out of painter's tape and covered head to toe in paint primer, hair tied up in a kerchief, glasses and work clothes on, I ran quickly to the local Wal-Mart to get some tape. As I was leaving the store, Bo Carter entered. Looking at his face, it registered in my psyche who was standing in front of me. I said hey and continued out of the store. He said hey and gave a slight wave and continued into the store. Walking toward my car, peace filled me. I was so overwhelmed at the healing power of Jesus. There was no rage, no anger, or bitterness. No shaky hands or queasy stomach. Not one negative emotion at all. Only God can so completely heal the heart and take away all residue of pain.

A friend of mine, Trevor Galpin, is an itinerant minister with

Fatherheart Ministries in Taupo Bay, New Zealand. He and his wife, Linda, travel the globe teaching Fatherheart Schools so people have an opportunity to receive a revelation of Father's love and learn how to live in a continuous experiential relationship of Father God loving us. At one such school, Trevor was teaching on heart forgiveness and made this comment, "When I forgive from my heart, my heart changes toward that person. With Holy Spirit's help, I can release that person from my unforgiveness and pour the cup of poison I've been drinking down the drain. Circumstances of life are just circumstances of life. Heart forgiveness doesn't mean the person changes or that the circumstance will change. It means you change."

Truly, I had changed.

How about you? Is there an experience of hurt that is as fresh today as the day it happened? Is there someone that you need to forgive from your heart?

I invite you to pray this prayer: *Jesus, I repent for making the pain of my past bigger than Your forgiveness. I repent for holding on to bitterness and unforgiveness. Jesus, I sever my agreement with bitterness. And I ask, Holy Spirit, that you would lift that root of bitterness up and out of me. Bitterness, I nail you to the cross of Jesus. I repent for being angry and responding to others out of my pain, hurt, anger and offenses. Jesus, what would you like to give me in exchange for bitterness?*

Be sure to write down what He gives you.

Holy Spirit, what lie have I believed that has allowed bitterness to fester in my heart?

Holy Spirit, when was the first time I partnered with bitterness? Holy Spirit, is there anyone I need to forgive for influencing me in this choice to partner with bitterness?

Heb. 12:14-15 Pursue peace with all men, and the sanctification without which no one will see the Lord. See to it that no one comes short of the grace of God; that no root of bitterness springing up causes trouble, and by it many be defiled;

Holy Spirit, is there anyone that has been defiled by this root of bitterness that I need to ask forgiveness of?

If He highlights someone to you, make note of their name and then choose a time to talk with them and ask forgiveness.

Holy Spirit, what lies do I believe that have allowed me to partner with anger and unforgiveness?

LIE:

Once you've written down every lie He shares with you, pray this prayer: *I renounce and break agreement with the lie that...*

Fill in the blank with the lies that He has revealed to you. Continue this prayer for each lie.

Holy Spirit, what's the truth?

TRUTH:

List the truth He shows you.

Do you need to forgive someone from the heart? Go ahead. You try it. If you need help, go back to the sections where we walked through forgiving our mother and our father and use that as a model for you. Just be real and let the words flow from your heart.

Jason Vallotton wrote in his book, *The Supernatural Power of Forgiveness*, "Part of forgiveness is acknowledging what is going on inside of you. Allow yourself to feel the weight of that perpetrated sin."

Be honest about how it made you feel. Be honest in communicating what their actions cost you. Ask Father God how He sees that person. Ask Him what lies you believe about them that are preventing you from seeing them the way He does. Renounce and break agreement with those lies. After counting the cost, forgive the person(s), then release and bless them.

As Holy Spirit encouraged me in that bible study, don't shrink back. If you endure this, there is joy on the other side. I do encourage you to write this process out on paper. I don't, however, encourage you to write it in your journal. When you're done, be done. Rip it up and throw it away. Don't have it there in writing to go back to ever again.

You were made in the image and likeness of God and He remembers our sins no more.[23] I encourage you to do the same.

If you need to do so, pray your forgiveness prayer before continuing.

---

23   Psalm 103:12

Chapter 15

Letting Go of the Pain

I had several experiences with extended family members growing up that felt like rejection, emotional distancing and just plain dislike. I never felt welcomed in my paternal grandmother's home, tolerated out of familial obligation, but not "I'm so excited to see you" welcomed. I felt like the dislike they had for my mom was passed on to me. I never experienced love, acceptance or any type of positive emotion inside my paternal grandmother's home. To be honest, I don't have one good memory of times spent there. I looked forward to our annual family reunion when people gathered there from different states. It was the only time I felt safe. The glares were hid discreetly behind the niceties of fellowship with distant relatives.

For years, even into adulthood, I managed my half of the relationship sending pictures of the kids here or there, going to visit for an hour when I came home. One day, as I sat in my Tennessee home reflecting on my childhood, I wondered if I would be missed if I just stopped going 'down to the house', as we called it. No one ever called me. No one ever sent cards or pictures to me. I felt like I was having a one sided relationship with people who could care less if I came around or not. So, I stopped visiting altogether.

But, I carried that rejection, that disapproval in my heart for a very long time. I can't tell you the number of times, I've chosen to forgive or the number of times I've repented for judging my paternal family or the number of times I've released them from my expectations of what family should be like, literally shredding into thousands of pieces every IOU I held against them.

One of the things I've come to know about Father God is that He aims His love at anything that stands in the way of you being completely transformed into the image and likeness of His dear Son, Jesus.

One day, in a moment of reflecting upon the injustices of my childhood, I wrote the word HATE in big letters and double underlined it on my paper. And then I began a journal rant, "I hate them. I hate who they are. I hate how they love. I hate their ridicule. I hate how they treat my mom. I hate that they don't change, won't change, don't care. I hate that they don't see how their behavior, their control damages our family."

No sooner than the words were out on paper did I realize that wasn't the truth. My heart no longer felt hatred towards them. So I wrote, "Father, I don't hate them. Father, forgive them for they know not what they do." And then I asked Father, what was all that? I've forgiven them.

And He said to me, "Those feelings are a familiar spirit. Those lies are the voice of the accuser." The evil one was trying to get me to go back and pick up those negative emotions as if Jesus never took them away. He almost tricked me into believing that they were mine.

Once Holy Spirit highlighted the evil one's scheme to me, I began to journal again, "Father, I forgive them for being unable to love me like I needed to be loved. I forgive them for their lies, for their maltreatment. I forgive them for trying to control everyone's life. I forgive myself for hating them, for not being able to trust them. From the heart, I forgive them. I am tearing up every I O U and I repent for being critical of them and for judging them. These are Your kids, God. And You love them. Father, give me Your eyes, Your heart for them. Let Your voice, Your words be louder in my spirit than the voice of the accuser. I've closed my heart to them. I don't know how to recapture what is lost. Truthfully, Father, I don't know if I want to." And again that old feeling welled up within me, "I HATE THEM," I railed.

"No, you don't," He said, "you hate the brokenness. You hate the puppetry. You hate that their eyes are blind. I grieve that too. I long for them to know me. I long to be discovered by them. Daughter, just make sure your boundaries aren't brick walls."

"I don't want to be in relationship with them," I said.

"No one is forcing you to be in relationship with them. Are you safe? Can you be vulnerable? Do you feel valued? Significant? You're not required to be in relationship with everyone in the world," Father said to me.

I then had the thought, "Just because you're born into a family doesn't make them family."

To which Father gently replied, "Even though it's my desire for you to be family. There's something I've placed in you, they need and something in them, you need. Beloved, love always requires a choice."

"Nah, I don't want that for myself," I admitted to God, "I can risk loving but it's not worth the risk."

Father God said to me, "Remember *Redeeming Love*?"[24]

To which I replied, "Yea, but everyone can't be Hosea."

Again Father whispered gently on my heart, "Love always requires a choice. How have I loved you?"

I answered, "While I was yet in sin, Christ died for me. Even when I couldn't love you back, you loved me."

Father said to me, "So why are you requiring something of them they can't give you?"

---

24 *Redeeming Love* is a fiction novel by Francine Rivers that retells the biblical account of the book Hosea.

I responded, "I'm not."

Father again, "And yet you're withholding love because of that."

I said to Him, "No, I'm just choosing to **NOT** be in relationship. There is no connection."

And Daddy God said to me, "There is the blood. Don't repay evil for evil, my beloved. Overcome evil with good."

"Hmmm," I replied, "so what does it look like to manage my love towards them in a way that honors You? How do I re-present You to them?"

Father said, "Are you doing this for Me or you?"

"Oh it would definitely be for you," I answered truthfully, "I'm not interested in a relationship with them."

"Why?" Father asked.

To Daddy God, I said, "Because I don't want to be around them." That was the nice answer. My heart said, "Cause I can't stand the sight of them."

Dad being Dad, who is more for something than He is against it doesn't even address my verbal or heart answer. He simply said, "Beloved, Love has no agenda. So what can you honor about them?"

To which I replied, "They love their family. They seem to be an incredibly tight knit group. I'm just not included. I don't feel loved by them. I feel nothing for them. I don't hate them. I don't have remorse or regret. I don't even feel numb. It's as if they are strangers. I've always been an outsider to them."

Father said, "Then love them like a stranger. How would you love a stranger?"

I said, "I would speak when spoken to. I might speak or wave or smile."

And Papa said to me, "My beloved, start with what you **CAN** do. I am the God of increase. I can take a meager lunch and feed thousands. I can take what you offer me and exponentially multiply it."

What was Truth teaching me as I encountered the loving correction of my Heavenly Father in this exchange? John 13:34 reads, "A new commandment I give to you, that you love one another; as I have loved you, that you also love one another." Father always manages His love towards us.

How has the Father loved you? That commandment didn't say love the people you like as I have loved you or love the people you get along with, as I have loved you. So, the question to me and the question to you, how has the Father loved you?

When you can let go of every expectation of what love in return should look like, you are free to love unconditionally.

So what does honor look like in the midst of dysfunction and toxic relationships? Ask God to give you an honoring thought. If that doesn't come to you, ask yourself, how would you honor a stranger? For me, the answer is easy. When I don't know someone and I want to honor them, I always ask Father how He sees that person. Then I love them through God's eyes as I hear what He says about them.

Why is this so easy to do for strangers and sometimes not as easy to do for those we are familiar with? I'm not sure. But I do know that Father hasn't loved me based on my performance. His love for me is far deeper than what I do or what I don't do. His love for me isn't based on me getting it right, saying the right things, or even reciprocating love to Him at the right moments. In all of my frailty, in all of my failings, in all of my successes, in all of my confidence, His love never fails. It never gives up on me. So, if I am to love as Father loves, what does that look like?

1 Corinthians 13 is definitely a great place to start. Does this mean

for me that I'm running back to my paternal family to reconcile? No, no it doesn't. It means I'm free to love them right where I am today. Reconciliation takes two. Just as I've made no effort to connect, neither have they. No connection equals no relationship.

The beautiful thing is that in letting go of the animosity and the pain, Father was able to fill my heart with more of His love. When I see them now, my hearts SWELLS with love. I'm genuinely HAPPY to see them. I'm not remembering wounds of a painful childhood, or perceived wrongs against my mom or I. None of that comes into play. I simply feel love for them. And yes, at times, I even MISS them. A lot of time has passed. I don't know how to be in relationship with them. But what I can do is start today where I am and enjoy the moments when I happen to be in the presence of my extended paternal family.

That doesn't sound like the "right" Christian thing to do or say, does it? Here again, the beautiful thing about freedom is that I'm free to begin again from where I am today. As Father loves me, I will be different. But today, I no longer have to pretend or do the right thing for the sake of doing the right thing. I can be true to me without pretense or falseness. It's okay to start where you are. Father knows the truth about you.

What Truth has taught me is that in conflict, it's not so much about the right thing or the wrong thing. For at all times, whether right or wrong, I am free to love. And with that revelation, I am committed to loving my extended family members. I am committed to seeing them and honoring them as Father sees them. I am committed to keep no record of wrong, which means I can no longer agree with the evil one every time they do something that reminds me of days gone by adding it to my proverbial scorecard of wrong doing. I am committed to suffer long and to be kind. I am committed to not behaving rudely or being provoked. I am committed to NOT thinking evil of my paternal family. I am committed to believe and hope that even in this, my relationship with my paternal family, reconciliation and restoration will come. I am committed to boundaries that don't look like brick walls. Most importantly, I am committed to loving as Father has loved me.

I don't hate them. I have forgiven from my heart. In my encounter with Truth, Holy Spirit empowered me with a plan to be more for love and honor than against being betrayed, rejected or hurt.

Truth also showed me that trust is an issue of the heart. While it's never easy to trust someone after you've been betrayed, I can choose to trust when I am completely secure in the One who heals all wounds. With His wisdom, I can put boundaries in place that define what I can do and what I can't do, what I will do and what I won't do. Those boundaries tell me what to do and I do it. They are not self-protection mechanisms or even elements to control or manipulate another person. When I am secure in the One who loves me, who protects me, who heals me, I can open my heart to love. I choose to give trust because of the condition of my heart, not the other person's. If I wait for someone to earn my trust, I am asking them to perform in a certain way to make me feel safe. The scary thing about someone acting in a certain manner, is that it's just that, an act. By choosing to give trust, I can express what I need and allow the other person the opportunity to manage their love in a way that says, "I hear you."

I once heard a speaker say, "When the threat of harm is high, the level of love is low." I saw my mom as a threat to my independence, my freedom, my right to be right, my right to parent and live a certain way, even my right to be a Christian the way I wanted to know God. Instead of being free to love, I always felt like I was protecting myself against being controlled or manipulated. I didn't trust her with my heart because I felt like she had never taken the time to know it.

Truth taught me that one of the ways Love manifests is self-control, which simply means I manage me. Because Father's love has been poured into my heart and healed me of those painful places from my past experiences with my mom, I no longer have to react out of the pain of my past experience. I am free to love. Freely I have received Father's love; freely I can give Father's love away.

The real question is do I want to pursue a relational connection with my mom? One day as I was riding in the car, Holy Spirit said to me, "Felicia, you're always encouraging people to see others through Father's eyes. Would you like to know how Father God sees your mom?" My immediate response was no. And I realized in that moment, that I had spent so much of my life not being a daughter and closing my heart off from her to keep it safe and protected that it was easier for me to continue that pattern than to begin again and risk disappointment.

I had silently bought into a lie about my mom and several other family members. And that lie was if you won't let me control you, I'll withhold my love from you. Because many of my past experiences said this was true, I chose distance as a boundary and only associated with my family as minimally as possible.

What I love, is that, as wrong as I was in my thought process and actions, Holy Spirit didn't chide me or make me feel bad. He never said anything more about it that day. But a few days later, He revisited the subject again shining His light on my ungodly belief and the wall I had erected in my heart towards my family.

As He did, I realized that the more God fills your life, the more freedom you have. I am free to simply love. And yes, disappointment may come. Pain and heartache may happen. It is a risk we take when we love. But Jesus is right there to take away your disappointment, pain and heartache and so fully love you that you can get up and begin again because love keeps no record of wrong.

So I opened my heart to Father God and I prayed this prayer: *"Father, I have no agenda here other than to love as You love. I believe it is Your desire to heal and restore my connection with my mom, with my extended family. I've all but closed the door. Papa, soften my heart. Give me Your love for her and for them. I receive Your grace to see them as You see them and to open my heart to reach out to them and embrace them."*

And so I'll ask you the questions Holy Spirit asked me on that day:

Can you after years of experiencing a history of pain, say yes, I love my mom? Yes, I love my family?

Can you be powerful? Can you choose to trust again? Can you respond in unconditional love? Can you choose to let go of fear and put on love? Are you willing to receive Father's grace to live pain free?

...More importantly, do you want to?

2 Cor. 5:18-19 Now all these things are from God, who reconciled us to Himself through Christ and gave us the ministry of reconciliation, namely, that God was in Christ reconciling the world to Himself, not counting their trespasses against them, and He has committed to us the word of reconciliation.

You're called to be a reconciler. How do we reconcile if we are counting their trespasses against them? Love keeps no record of wrong. Beloved, it's time to tear up the scorecard.

Rom. 12:18 (Mirror Bible) *"You have within you what it takes to be everyone's friend regardless of how they treat you."*

With Holy Spirit's help, I recognized that I was believing the lie that I didn't feel valued enough to be known; significant enough to be heard and not worthy of their time. So my response was just to cut them off and not deal with them at all.

However, I am 100% responsible for me. I can't control or change what my relatives think or feel about me. But I can control me. And I don't have to respond to wounding with more wounding. I can break the cycle. I can choose to forgive. I can choose to love.

What will you choose? Will you continue to respond from pain or will you choose to forgive and love?

When we forgive, we cancel the offense of the wound. The issue of the love deficit must still be addressed. This is the issue that was resurfacing in my heart with my extended family members. My heart was still void of the love I so desired from them. And in that hole, I came into agreement with many negative emotions.

When Father comes into that place in my heart, His love fills that void. Many people are still left wanting. Only Father's love is enough to so completely fill a void that you become healed, whole and transformed.

If you struggle with relational dynamics in your personal, immediate, or extended family, I pray you will grab a hold of the wisdom of Holy Spirit, the love of Father God, and the all sufficient grace that Jesus' blood provides for us to love even as you are loved by Father.

Can you relate? Have you experienced rejection or relational dysfunction in your relationship with family members?

Maybe you're saying, but Felicia, you can't possibly know what they did to me? You can't possibly be telling me to put myself in a position to be hurt again. I'm telling you no such thing. Each person has to walk through their own healing journey inside of their relationship with Father, Jesus and Holy Spirit. There is no formula or cookie cutter method to healing.

What I am asking you to do is trust the Godhead with your heart. I am asking you to seek the counsel of Holy Spirit, ask Him what you should do, what your next step is.

A powerful person knows what they can do and what they can't do; what they will do and what they won't do. Don't do something because you think it's the right thing to do. That is being motivated by the fear of man. Let every decision you make, every action you undertake be motivated by love.

Let's pray together: *Father God, I repent for choosing to walk in anger/hatred instead of love. I repent for not seeing my family members the way You see them. I repent for keeping a record of their wrongs. I repent for wanting them to pay for their misdeeds. I repent for perceiving them as a threat to my safety. I repent for allowing the fear of pain and disappointment to paralyze me from loving my family well. Father, I forgive my family members. I forgive them for not being able to love me the way I needed to be loved. I forgive them for not seeing me, hearing me, embracing me. I forgive them for making me feel like an outcast, the black sheep of the family and I release them from every IOU. I release them from every expectation of what family should be like. I bless them, Father, each one of them. May they become all that You have destined them to be. Father, heal and restore my connection with my family and soften my heart to love like You love. I hand You rejection. I hand You anger. I hand You resentment. I hand You bitterness. I hand You disappointment. What would You like to give me in exchange?*

Be sure to record what you are given in the divine exchange.

Now let's ask: *Holy Spirit, what lies have I believed about my family?*

Holy Spirit, what other feelings, lies or ungodly beliefs have I owned as mine that are really the evil one masquerading as a familiar spirit?

LIE:

Once you've written down every lie He shares with you, pray this prayer: *I renounce and break agreement with the lie that...*

Fill in the blank with the lies that He has revealed to you. Continue this prayer for each lie.

Holy Spirit, what's the truth?

TRUTH:

List the truth He shows you.

Finally, let's ask Papa: *Father God, how do You see my family?*

Be sure to record what He gives you.

CHAPTER 16

EMBRACING CHILDLIKENESS

Matt. 18:3 ...Truly I say to you, unless you are converted and become like children, you will not enter the kingdom of heaven.

In November 2008, I wrote in the pages of my journal, "More than anything in the world, I love being Your little girl. I love knowing that You love me. I love feeling secure in You. I love knowing that I am wanted, that You value me. Thanks, Papa. You are my Heavenly Daddy and I adore You."

One of the most exhilarating characteristics of Father God's nature is that He is a Redeemer. Not having had much of a childhood growing up, I had nothing to draw on in the way of merriment, fun, dependency or simply being loved and carefree. So Jesus, in my time with Him, started giving me visions of children playing and experiencing life. He would share these encounters with me and invite me to observe not only the child but also the loving heartfelt response of the parent to their child so I could begin to understand how Father God responds to me.

In my first lesson from the life of a little one, Truth taught me about the "boo boo." With worship music playing softly in my bedroom one morning, I began to hear, in my head, the sound of children laughing. I inhaled, closed my eyes and immediately saw a little one playing on the merry go round in a playground. The little tot was laughing and having a blast when all of a sudden, her hand slipped from the bar and she fell to the ground.

Immediately, she looked at her scarred hands, began to cry and ran to her mother. "Kiss it Mommy. Kiss it," the little tot demanded. The mom stopped her conversation, kissed the little tot's hands, hugged her tight and said, "I'm so sorry you were hurt. Are you going to be okay?" With a nod, the tot said yes and off she skipped back to the playground.

As this vision faded from my mind's eye, I thought of all of my unkissed boo boos. I thought of how my mom would have responded so differently from the mom in this vision. And then, I thought of humanities unkissed boo boos as well: the child who died too young, the sibling who lied on us, the friend who betrayed us, the husband who left us, the salesman who cheated us, the broken heart, the barren womb, the list of boo boos goes on and on. Instantly from the Spirit of Truth, I gained understanding that has never left me.

Father God never desires that we grow pass the point of coming to Him. Yet, we tend to run away from our Heavenly Daddy instead of to Him. Even now, it's Abba's desire for us to bring our scars to Him and receive His assurance and healing touch. On our physical bodies, scar tissue never grows. When we skin our knee as a little tot, even though we grow and mature, the area around that skinned knee stays the same, the reminder of the damage visible by the scar on the epidermis. If our hearts remain scarred, we will never grow or mature past the point of that wounded place. And though no visible reminder exists that we can observe with our natural eye, our jaded response to life and to people is a clear indication that a scar remains over that hurtful place.

Father's desire is to pour love into our heart so that all of those pains, memories, hurt feelings, and carts of baggage that we have stuffed away inside begin to rise to the surface like sediment. Even now, He longs for us to sit at His feet and allow the pain to be poured out onto Jesus. After all, this is why He died. His love is the balm that heals every scar, washing over us and growing us past the point of responding to life through our pain and hurtful places.

Is. 53:5 He was wounded for our transgressions, He was bruised for our iniquities.

When gold is purified in the fire, the heat causes the sediments and impurities to rise to the top. The goldsmith comes along and skims off the dross. I believe this is why John the Baptist said Jesus would baptize us in the Holy Spirit and fire.[25] The refining fire of God's love purifies us. After all, we are His workmanship.[26] Father God pours His love into our hearts and dislodges all the hidden pain we have stuffed deep inside our souls where we hope no one will ever discover it. He doesn't dislodge the hidden pain to cause you more pain from remembering. The pain is dislodged so that it will come up and out, skimmed off by God.

We bring our boo boos to Him as our Father because He desires us to come to Him and say, "Kiss it, Daddy. Kiss it." And He does. When you receive the Father's love into the depths of who you are, His love begins to heal and transform all of those unhealed and broken places.

Prov. 23:7 As a man thinketh in his heart, so is he.

If you believe that your pain is too big for God then every time you get a boo boo, you will run from Him. When you begin to experience God's love, you understand that with one kiss, He can make the pain go away. Even now Father God is saying to you, "Bring Me your boo boo, let Me kiss them. Let Me heal them."

Prov. 4:23 Keep your heart with all diligence for out of it flows the issues of life.

Our adultness tells us to run away, to cover ourselves, to use fig leaves for bandages and hide. Little tots just believe that Mommy and Daddy can make it all better. They trust without question. That's what God wants from you – to believe that He, your Heavenly Daddy can and will make it all better. He wants you to trust Him without question, though I must add, He's absolutely not afraid of your questions. He wants us all to come to a place where we are so resolute in the character and nature of who He is that this issue of whether or not we can trust Him will forever be settled. So bring your boo boos to Him and let Him

---

25   Matthew 3:11
26   Ephesians 2:10

kiss them.

What about you? Are there boo boos that you need to bring to Father God? If so, I invite you to pray this prayer with me:

Father God, I repent for running from You instead of running to You. I repent for not dealing with my hurts. I forgive (the people) that have contributed to these hurts, pains, wounds and offenses.

Holy Spirit, what are the unhealed hurts that I've tucked away so I don't have to deal with them?

Holy Spirit, what are the lies I have believed that have kept these hurts from being healed?

LIE:

Once you've written down every lie He shares with you, pray this prayer: *I renounce and break agreement with the lie that...*

Fill in the blank with the lies that He has revealed to you. Continue this prayer for each lie.

Holy Spirit, what's the truth?

TRUTH:

List the truth He shows you.

Father God, with childlike faith, I come to receive your healing touch. I invite You to pour Your love in every unhealed place. Kiss it, Daddy, kiss it.

CHAPTER 17

FINDING JOY IN A BOUQUET OF ADVERSITY

In another adventure with Truth, He taught me the lesson of the weeds. As I encountered Truth this day, I found myself in my favorite childhood park. Spring was in the air and the landscape was awash with the beauty of flowers bursting forth with vibrant color. I observed a little tot fascinated with the spectacular array of all the flowers in bloom. Admonished by her mommy not to pick the flowers because they were there for everyone to enjoy, the little tot grabbed the hand her mother was offering her and toddled along still wistfully looking back at the beautiful display of bright colors. Deeper into the park, the mom located a spot to spread her blanket and commenced to setting out the picnic lunch she had brought along for the family to enjoy.

The toddler wandered into the grass and seeing "yellow flowers" full of color, like those big ones by the entrance, she began to pluck one for her mommy. After plucking a few more, her little hands now full, she toddled back over to her mom and said with delight, "Look Mommy! For you. For you." Smiling really big, she handed her mommy the bouquet of "flowers".

As her mom looked at the dandelions, she smiled with great joy, received the flowers from her little tot, and reached down to give her the biggest hug and kiss on the cheek. With a laugh in her throat, the mom said to her tot, "Thank you, little one, for my flowers." Finding a paper cup in the picnic basket, the mom proceeded to place the dandelions in her makeshift vase and used them as a centerpiece for the family lunch.

I realized that I was observing this scene with bated breath waiting to see how the mom would respond. See my mom would have thrown the weeds on the ground and scolded me or popped me for straying away from her and bringing her weeds. And in searching my own heart, I had to admit that my reaction to my own children would have been far less grand. I would have taken the dandelions from my child and then when she wasn't looking, I would have discarded them. Either response depicts an uncaring parent who isn't sincerely interested in the gift her child has brought. And this was my perception of Father God - uncaring, ruthless, heartless. Oh, I had layered this perception under mounds and mounds of Hallelujahs and good Christianese so no one would have ever known this was my assessment of God. Truth wasn't interested in deception. He was there to bring me into a right revelation of His Father in how I perceived and experienced Him.

I learned that day that Father is not afraid of my weeds. He delights in me bringing them to Him. So much so, that He creates a banqueting table for me in the presence of my enemies and He uses my dandelions as the centerpiece.

As this scene faded from my imagination, Truth said to me, "Felicia, does your weeds look like flowers? Can you bring your bouquet of weeds to Father trusting that He will receive them with great joy and delight?"

I paused. What do my weeds look like? Do I see them as beautiful and vibrant? Or are they strangling the life out of me? Jesus was asking me if I could look at my weeds - my circumstances, my crises, my present situation and marvel at them in the same light as a little one does. Wow.

James 1:2a Consider it all joy, my brethren, when you encounter various trials.

John 16:33 (NIV) *In this world you will have trouble. But take heart! I have overcome the world.*

All the weeds do is show my response to life. Am I consistent? Am I at peace? Do I maintain my integrity? Do I remain constant in who I believe God is when the weeds surface? How do I think? How do I behave when the weeds – my circumstances, crises, and present situation – surface?

My weeds are there simply, for me, as the beloved, to learn to know by experience that I indeed have the mind of Christ and that Father's love has absolutely transformed me to behave as He would no matter the situation or circumstance.

I can be glad, even in the midst of my weeds, because I understand that the trying of my conviction (what I believe to be true) produces constancy. As His daughter (son), I am complete in Him. And if I remain steadfast, when the undertaking of it is brought to its end, I will stand in the living revelation of *Romans 8:28, "And we know that God causes all things to work together for good to those who love God, to those who are called according to His purpose."*

And there we will see Father, beaming with great delight, "Oh! Look at this beautiful bouquet. Look at how you responded with My mind, My heart, My perspective. Such a delightful centerpiece for our banqueting table!"

James 1:2-4 Consider it all joy, my brethren, when you encounter various trials, knowing that the testing of your faith produces endurance. And let endurance have its perfect result, so that you may be perfect and complete, lacking in nothing.

Even though the storm was raging on the sea, Jesus slept while the disciples in their adultness looked at the weeds (in their case, the storm) and feared greatly.[27] Strength and courage flow from an awareness that God is with us.[28] For truly that is the delight and blessedness of the incarnation of Jesus. Immanuel, God with us, bringing His peace on earth among men with whom He is pleased.[29]

Challenges are an opportunity to experience God giving generously to us His peace in the midst of our darkness. Our weeds allow us to

---

27 Luke 8:23
28 Matthew 1:23
29 Luke 2:14

see the bigness of God and witness His delight towards us. They are an opportunity to see His goodness demonstrated in our lives as our hellish situations spread out before Him as a bouquet on His banqueting table.

What about you? Have you ever picked "flowers" for your Mother? Or perhaps you've had one of your own children pick "flowers" for you. What was your mother's response? What was your response to your children?

If necessary, stop for a moment and work through any issues of forgiveness. Forgive your mom for not honoring the gift you presented her. Forgive her for making you feel as if she didn't care. If you were the mom or dad who has done that to a child, forgive yourself for not honoring them. Forgive yourself for making your child think you didn't care about them or didn't take the time to notice them. Then, release yourself or your mom from your judgments and injured expectations.

How do you believe Father God would respond to you if you handed Him your weeds?

Can you smile at your circumstances and declare God's kingdom come and Father's will be done? Perhaps at times, as I also did, you still see God has an angry judge instead of a loving Father who cares about what you care about.

Let me encourage you with a truth Holy Spirit taught me about Father God. When Jesus saw Mary and Martha's grief over the death of their brother Lazarus, what did He do?

John 11:35 Jesus wept.

Why did He weep? I believe Jesus wept because He saw His Father weeping. And I believe Lazarus wasn't the first person Father, Jesus and Holy Spirit have wept over. My heart fully believes that many times Father has wept alongside His children who are experiencing grief and weeping. It is imperative that we, as Father's children, know that the things that concern us concern Him. He is not an uncaring, absent Father. He is the Dad who is there. He is ever present.

How can you be so sure of that, you might ask?

John 5:19 "The son can do nothing of himself. I only do what I see the Father doing; I only say what I hear Father saying".

Too far a stretch? Try this one:

Hebrews 1:3 "The Son radiates God's own glory and expresses the very character of God..."

In the midst of our weeds, He has given us His peace – *"My peace I give to you, My peace I leave with you, not as the world gives. Let not your heart be troubled, neither let it be afraid."*[30]

Why? Because out of your heart flows the issues of life.[31] If your heart is troubled or full of fear, guess what your outlook on life will be? God wants you to know that you can experience His peace, you can walk in His peace, you can live in His peace even when the weeds threaten to overtake you. When you know the depth of His love for you, and the all surpassing greatness of His power, you can look at the weeds of your circumstances and smile. After all, they are just a beautiful bouquet of flowers in the hands of a loving and very good Father.

Can you count it all joy knowing that Father wants to give you His beauty in the midst of your weeds?

If your answer to that question is no, I invite you to pray this prayer with me: *Jesus, I hand you my colored lenses of negativity and disillusionment.*

I know Jesus is within you and you are one with Him but for the sake of the divine exchange happening here in the spirit realm, I'm going to ask you to bear with me. I'd like to suggest that you physically take a moment, reach up to your eyes and as a prophetic act, symbolically remove the lenses or "pretend glasses" from your face and hand them to Jesus by holding the "glasses" in your hand and extending them outward

---

30   John 14:27
31   Proverbs 4:23

releasing the glasses from your hand.

Once you've done that, ask Jesus, *What would you like to give me in exchange?*

Be sure to record what Jesus gave you in exchange for negativity and disillusionment.

If you've seen God differently than He desires you to see Him, I invite you to pray this prayer with me. Feel free to insert your own words that describe how you are seeing Father God.

Father God, I repent for judging You. I repent for seeing You as harsh, uncaring, and ruthless. Give me a right perspective of who You are and how You desire me to experience You. Father God, here is my bouquet of weeds (take a moment to tell Father God about any crisis or circumstances that you are facing at the present moment).

Then ask: *Holy Spirit, what are the lies I believe about my present circumstances?*

LIE:

Once you've written down every lie He shares with you, pray this prayer: *I renounce and break agreement with the lie that...*

Fill in the blank with the lies that He has revealed to you. Continue this prayer for each lie.

Holy Spirit, what's the truth?

TRUTH:

List the truth He shows you.

I'd like to end by releasing a blessing over you. These are the words Truth spoke into my heart that morning long ago as the encounter in my favorite childhood park began to fade from my mind's eye. So I bless you and release this truth deep into your innermost being:

"Beloved, just as I endured the cross for the joy that was set before Me, fellowship with Me in your suffering and count it all joy, knowing that I have your back. I am working it all out for good. Shod your feet with the preparation of the gospel of peace. May you experience the joy of Father's God provision and protection as you rest in My peace in the midst of your weeds."

CHAPTER 18

THE BEAUTY OF TRUST:
NOW I LAY ME DOWN TO SLEEP

In yet another encounter, Truth took me back to a fond memory of Brittany, our oldest daughter. When Britt was little, our favorite book to read at bedtime was *Goodnight Moon*. To this day, some twenty plus years later, she owns a copy of that book and I can still recite almost the entire book from rote memory.

As I was lying with Jesus, I saw Brittany and I in her bedroom going through our bedtime ritual. I read *Goodnight Moon* to her. Then together on our knees, we recited the twenty-third Psalm. She prayed. I pulled back the cover and into the bed she climbed. I tucked her in, gave her a goodnight kiss, switched on the night-light and left the room turning off the overhead light on my way out the door. It never ceased to amaze me how often Britt would fall fast asleep as soon as she was tucked in.

As the memory of tucking Britt in faded from my mind's eye, Holy Spirit started speaking to my heart, "How many times have you watched your children fall asleep? They have an amazing ability to simply lay their head on their pillow and fall fast asleep. They aren't trying to figure out how things are going to work out for the next day, what they will wear or what they will eat. Without even thinking about it or thinking on it, they just fall asleep. Thinking about those things is the parent's responsibility. Felicia, Father wants you to be like that."

I felt impressed to pick up my Bible and find the scripture about the lilies. Using the word 'lilies' as a cross-reference in my interlinear, I was directed to *Matthew 6:25-34*. *"For this reason I say to you, do not be worried about your life, {as to} what you will eat or what you will drink; nor for your body, {as to} what you will put on. Is not life more than food, and the body more than clothing? Look at the birds of the air, that they do not sow, nor reap nor gather into barns, and {yet} your heavenly Father feeds them. Are you not worth much more than they? And who of you by being worried can add a {single} hour to his life? And why are you worried about clothing? Observe how the lilies of the field grow; they do not toil nor do they spin, yet I say to you that not even Solomon in all his glory clothed himself like one of these. But if God so clothes the grass of the field, which is {alive} today and tomorrow is thrown into the furnace, {will He} not much more {clothe} you? You of little faith! Do not worry then, saying, 'What will we eat?' or 'What will we drink?' or 'What will we wear for clothing?' For the Gentiles eagerly seek all these things; for your heavenly Father knows that you need all these things. But seek first His kingdom and His righteousness, and all these things will be added to you. So do not worry about tomorrow; for tomorrow will care for itself. Each day has enough trouble of its own."*

Holy Spirit continued, "Father wants you to know without a shadow of a doubt or concern that provision is His job not yours. It is His great pleasure to provide for His children. No good thing will He withhold from them that walk uprightly. His desire is that you cease from striving and worry long enough to know that He is God. He will clothe you, He will feed you."

I realized that Holy Spirit was speaking truth to me, a truth that would completely transform me once I believed it and began to live from it. But there were so many issues in my heart that wrestled with this truth - lack, fear of abandonment, self-reliance, mistrust and a poverty mindset. All of these things were preventing me from really taking the Lord at His Word. I would plan, worry, control and manipulate. I wasn't doing the best job at being God but I was trying really hard.

As I saw the things that hindered me from receiving this truth into every part of me, I asked Holy Spirit, "What must I do to believe?" He replied, "Felicia, what Father really wants is to heal those places in your heart so you can take Him at His Word and truly begin to lay your head on your pillow at night without thinking about what's next. When did God provide manna for the children of Israel?" "At night," I responded, "while the children were resting.[32] They would wake up and it was there clinging to the dew waiting for them." "That's correct," Holy Spirit encouraged, "as you rest in the Lord, He provides. If you'd like, Jesus can take those things that are preventing you from receiving the fullness of this truth into your heart. He's already died for them." And so, I handed Jesus worry, planning, manipulation, self-reliance, fear, doubt and control. As I did, I immediately saw a picture of me nursing my children when they were babes.

As my kids nursed, they would often fall asleep. As they fell asleep, they would pull away from the breast with their little mouths wide open. A little milk would still be at the corner of their mouths and they would just rest, safe and secure in my arms – sleeping and resting without a care in the world.

Ps 22:9 Yet You are He who brought me forth from the womb; You made me trust {when} upon my mother's breasts.

Holy Spirit said to me, "Felicia, there is a picture in that verse that is so key to your relationship with Father. Abba is El Shaddai, the mighty breasted One. Father wants you to come to Him and receive nourishment and the rich nutrients that come from nursing at His breast. He wants you to curl up in the cradle of His arm and drink of Him. He wants to fill you to the full so like a little babe, you can lay your head back in the crook of His arm and rest, safely, securely, without a care in the world. It's total reliance on the Father. That's how Jesus lives. That's how babies live. That's how He wants you to live and relate to Him as Father."

For the life of me, I couldn't fathom anything more unbelievable and inconceivable! I mean, my spirit knew this was true. But for most of my life, I had lived incongruent to such thoughts. I got my first job at

---

32   Numbers 11:9

fifteen. I worked a full time job from the time I was sixteen years old, working production in a local factory from four in the afternoon until midnight. I purchased my first car with my own funds. I paid for my own clothes. I had lived so independently looking out for "number one" pretty much all of my teenage and young adult life. I held no recollection of one tender moment with either parent. I had always lived an orphan lifestyle. At an early age, I closed my heart to being a daughter to my mom and dad and embraced my orphan-ness. So I struck out on my own at seventeen and decided to just live for myself. I felt like I couldn't please them anyway, so why try.

When one closes their heart to being parented, it's not like you know that is what you are doing. It isn't something I admit with pride. And yet, as James Jordan states in his book, *Sonship*, the orphan spirit is the root of all humanity's struggles(Jordan, 2012). To be alone, independent, without a father, striving to make a name for one's self, this is the essence of being an orphan.

My parents are both alive and even though I lived under their roof until I was seventeen years of age, I did not allow either of them to parent me. In my mom's words, I gave them hell. They couldn't tell me anything. It's like in my heart I had said, "I will have no parent over me. I will be my own authority." I didn't think they loved me so I didn't care diddly about what they thought. I no longer asked their permission to come or go. I no longer held them with any regard, reverence or respect. I had no value for their advice or opinion. In fact, if they offered one, I was most certainly going to do the complete opposite to what they advised. I had been my mom's helper, her servant but never her daughter. I didn't even know how to be a daughter if I tried.

When I tried to tell my mom things of the heart, she blabbed them to all of her friends so I stopped sharing my life with her. I didn't trust her to keep my confidence. My relationship with my dad was very perfunctory. We talked sports, current events, cars and little else. I just had no clue how to be parented. And to be honest, I had such a negative connotation of what a parent did and who a parent was that I had no desire for such a thing in my life, from God or from my earthly parents.

Extremely independent, I believed the lie that I didn't need anyone to survive. I alone was enough. I lived without a sense of identity. I lived in insecurity. I lived fighting for whatever I could get or whatever I believed was mine. Extremely selfish, I was often comparing what I had or didn't have to what someone else had. Afraid of what people thought of me, I hid the fear by being critical and judgmental. Even though I felt inferior, I spoke with great bravado always needing to be right.

So you can imagine how foreign this was for me to understand, how unfamiliar a concept words like rest, security, safety, and not a care in the world sounded to my ears. I didn't have any frame of reference with which my little girl, teenage or womanly heart could grasp such a thing.

Has there been a time in your life where you've closed your heart to being a son or a daughter to your parents? Maybe as you've grown into adulthood, life has thrown you so many curveballs that you've felt like you had to manage all on your own. Perhaps you still find yourself plotting and planning, like me, living in the world of robbing Peter to pay Paul just to make ends meet; always feeling like there was more month than money. I couldn't fathom just trusting some unseen God to handle my affairs. Can you relate?

If so, let's pray this prayer together:

Father, I repent for closing my heart to being a son/daughter to my parents. I repent for being independent and self-reliant. I repent for believing the lie that I didn't need anyone, not even my parents. I repent for believing the lie that my parents weren't worthy of my love, worthy of my respect, worthy of my honor. I repent for being hard-hearted and rebellious towards my parents. I repent for trusting in myself more than I've trusted in You. I repent for allowing fear to motivate my actions. I repent for partnering with control and manipulation whether knowingly or unknowingly. I repent for not trusting You.

Holy Spirit, I don't know how to be a son/daughter. But You are the greatest Teacher I know. Holy Spirit, would You teach me what it means to be interdependent? Would You show me how to live in utter reliance on

Father God? And would You make Your love so great and so real towards me that doing so isn't a hard thing? Would You teach me how to live from rest? For indeed it was You that has caused me to trust upon Your breast.

Would You come alongside me and teach me how to be parented by Father God? Would You teach me about sonship that I might live in right relationship with my Heavenly Father as You empower me to do so? Father God, I choose, in childlike faith, to be parented by You. Would You come and parent me now? Mom, Dad, I ask you to forgive me for closing my heart to you. I ask you to forgive me for not valuing you, for not honoring and respecting you. I ask you to forgive me for not believing the best about you, for not believing the best about us. Holy Spirit, would You begin to soften my heart towards my parents and help me see them the way Father God sees them?

Holy Spirit, how have I embraced an orphan lifestyle? What lies have I believed?

Be sure to record what He shows you. Then pray: *I renounce and break agreement with the lie that…*

Now ask: *Holy Spirit, what do I need to hand You to let go of my orphan ways?*

After recording what He gives you, pray this prayer: *Holy Spirit, I hand You…*(give to Him whatever it is He said you needed to let go of).

What would You like to give me in exchange?

Now, let's go after the lies: *Holy Spirit, what lies am I believing about my relationship with my parents?*

Holy Spirit, what lies have I believed that have prevented me from living as a son (daughter)?

LIE:

Once you've written down every lie He shares with you, pray this prayer: *I renounce and break agreement with the lie that...*

Fill in the blank with the lies that He has revealed to you. Continue this prayer for each lie.

Holy Spirit, what's the truth?

TRUTH:

List the truth He shows you.

Finally, let's ask Holy Spirit two very important questions to help reframe our thinking.

1) Holy Spirit, what does living from rest look like for me?

2) Holy Spirit, how do I begin to trust You with all of me?

Don't forget to write down your answers!

Chapter 19

An Expression of His Love

Truth, however, in all of His great love for me, knew just the picture that would help me relate to being parented by Father God. As I sat with Him, He took the opportunity to reacquaint me with what it means to be parented by showing me how our very own children relate to us. Each one of them responds differently to the love that Doug and I give them.

Our love is the same. We have always loved them. We have loved them from the beginning. They are the expression of the love that Doug and I share. They represent the oneness of our heartbeat and yet, because of their uniqueness, each responds very differently to the sameness of our love.

Brittany, our oldest, is very secure in our love. She's confident. She's funny. She knows who she is. She can go and be who she is because she is sure of our love. When she needs our help or advice she comes back for that but she knows that she is loved. We've watched Brittany excel and achieve amazing feats because of that confidence. She is an Ivy League graduate, highly sought after for her leadership capabilities and beginning life on her own as a young adult woman.

Our oldest son, Tre', is the intimate, cuddly one. When he's in our presence, you will most likely find him on our lap, hugging us, holding our hand, bending his cheek down for a kiss. He's learned well how to manage his freedom and what to do with the fruit of the Spirit called self-control.

This has been a process. He's had a paradigm shift about his parents. We parented from unhealed places before receiving a revelation of Father's love and goodness. As a result, Tre's view of God as Father changed as well. So even though he loves intimacy, there were times when he was unsure about what to do with not having a punisher or an enforcer. By nature, his temperament is more black and white, so he is at home with rules. Because we don't have a lot of hard fast rules, sometimes in the process of learning how to manage his freedom and himself, he messed up. Even though he made wrong choices, it didn't change our love for him. Neither did it affect how we give and show love to him.

Is that hard? Very! We're not Papa God. But one truth we all have gleaned on the God journey is that love is structure in which freedom is governed. Just as the banks of a river provide the boundaries that contain the water in the river, love becomes the boundaries that contain our freedom. We don't go around splashing our freedoms over the banks of love.

It's been amazing to watch Tre' as he learns to manage his freedoms inside the banks of love. Essentially what it means is that he has went from being someone who needed to be externally handled and controlled to someone who is learning to use internal guidance through his relationship with Father, Jesus and Holy Spirit to rule over his own city very well.

Our youngest daughter, Chaya is outspoken. She is a socially, bubbly extrovert. Her name in Hebrew means choose life and she has definitely chosen life to the full. As such, she makes a demand on you for love. She demands attention. "Hey look at me, I'm here. Hello world, listen to me." She reminds me of the friend in Luke 11 who kept knocking and knocking until the man got out of bed and answered. Chaya is like that. She is persistent in her demand for her presence to be known and yet extremely confident in who she is. She is not demanding in a needy, craving attention sort of way. In fact, she has a larger than life, vibrant personality that tends to fill a room. She's such a dominant leader that when Chaya is in a room, you're gonna know it. Chaya's confidence says, "I have a voice and my opinion matters." She has no trouble clearly articulating what's on her mind.

Our youngest, Jeremiah used to be timid and unsure. Still very quiet and reserved, he's a natural leader, a gifted orator, a talented actor, singer, and has an incredibly brilliant mind. Yet, there are times when he withholds himself or won't speak up and ask for things he needs or wants.

For a long time, he wasn't sure if it was okay to come and get a hug or a kiss. You could tell that he wanted affection but he wasn't sure if the risk of rejection was worth reaching out for affirmation. We often found him on the periphery not engaged in conversation or the liveliness that is known as the Murrell home.

Once in a store, I knew he wanted something and I had purposed in my heart that I would buy it for him if he asked. You could see him look at the object. Then he kind of looked at me. He put his hands in his mouth, looked back at the item, but he never asked. I was willing him to ask me for the object, rooting for him to speak up. And as much as I wanted to give him what he desired that day, because he didn't ask, I did not.

Over time, as Father has loved Jeremiah and he has experienced the safety of being himself in our home, his attitude about affection began to change. He now willingly comes for hugs and allows me to give him a kiss or a back rub, even pausing to hold my hand. He's also gotten better about asking for things he wants, trusting that we love him and that we won't withhold good if it's in our power to do so.

A beautiful thing for me is seeing how love transformed Jeremiah's once quiet and timid voice into one of confidence. Now, you often find him amongst his dad and siblings expressing his opinion and offering wisdom and insight on current events and other things that happen in and around our lives.

We have four children that are completely different from one another. They are all leaders in their own right and yet each one of them responds to us completely different. Just as all of my children are completely different from one another and just as they respond differently in their love to us and in their receiving of love from us, it is imperative that you grasp the universalness of this truth. All of us are God's children. We are all different. He never intended for us to be the same. This is why there is no cookie cutter formula for intimacy with God. You are going to receive and respond to love differently than someone else, because you're you. His love is the same for us all, but He never intended our relationships with Him to be one size fits all. It's His desire to live with you inside of your unique to you relationship.

So you've been introduced to our unique to us kids, our beloved children in whom we are well pleased. We aren't pleased with them because of anything they've done, though their achievements, year after year, completely astound me. We are pleased with them because they are a part of us, an extension of our love.

From a little nursing babe to present day, our hearts remain connected. Why are their lives filled with safety, security, confidence and happiness? It is because they've allowed themselves to be parented and on my breast, they learned to trust.

And while I could never understand being parented through the dysfunction of my personal parent child relationships, Truth used my own kids to show me what it looked like to be parented by Papa God. And I could hear Father cheering me on, "My child, you are the love that flows between My Son and I. Keep that milk breath!"

Just as my kids are the expression of love that flows from Doug and I, you are the love that flows between Father and Jesus. The Father wants a Bride for His only begotten Son. The Son wants to give the Father many more sons. The Father says to the Son, here's Your betrothed. The Son says to the Father, here are Your sons. And you are that expression of love. In this upside down kingdom, only through the heart, the faith, and the eyes of a child can you see and grasp this wonderful, simple expression of love.

Matthew 18:3 Except you become as little children, you will be no means enter the kingdom of heaven.

It's time to become young again. Being childlike is how we mature in God's kingdom. I bless you to hear Father saying to you, "Sleep now, little one. I will feed you. I will clothe you. Ah, yes! I love the smell of milk on your breath. You can trust in Me. You can rest safely and securely in Me. I love you. You can totally rely on, adhere to and be confident in My goodness."

CHAPTER 20

WHICH CHILD ARE YOU?

Like Brittany, are you confident? Do you know God loves you? Not just in your head know because a preacher told you or because the Bible told you, but know in your heart know because you have personally experienced His love.

When you receive an impartation of Father's love in this manner, you can go and do the same works that Jesus did and even greater works. All that Jesus did was because He knew who He was. His being directed His doing. Jesus lived loved and He gave away the love of Father God to others by releasing peace over stormy seas, sharing words of wisdom and life with others, healing the sick, cleansing the lepers, casting out demons, raising the dead, providing bread to the hungry and water to the thirsty. Like Jesus, you know how to steal away for time alone to come sit at the Father's feet and commune with Him. As such there is a confidence about you, a sense of authority.

Are you intimate like Tre'? Do you love to touch the heart of God, love to hold His hands and walk with Him in the cool of the day, love to curl up in His lap and just be with Him?

Or maybe like Tre's alter ego, you find yourself saying, I want this; I want to experience more of God, more of His love and yet there is still a part of you that clings to the traditions of men, legalism, rules, enforcers, and punishers. Perhaps freedom seems scary at first glance, a bit too much. Perhaps you have been so dominated by control to the degree that you don't know how to enjoy the freedom of your life in Christ. Or do you find yourself, like the children of Israel, saying no Moses you go talk to Him? Just tell me what He says for me to do and I will do it. I'd rather have rules than relationship.

If you need rules to help you feel safe, let me encourage you, embrace the law of love. The greatest "law" Jesus gave us was to love the Lord your God with all of your heart, soul and mind. The key for you is to fall as hopelessly, and utterly in love with the Godhead as He is with you.

True love creates devotion. It breeds commitment and fuels integrity. I would never want to hurt, grieve or disappoint the One or one I love. Alignment happens inside the union of our love relationship.

If you can identify with Tre's alter ego, I invite you to pray this prayer with me: *Father God, You said that it was for freedom that you've set us free. Would You come and fill my heart so completely with love that I can move from being in love with law to living by the law of love? Would You align my heart with Yours? I repent for clinging to traditions, legalism, rules, and the right thing to do. I repent for exalting these things over receiving Your love and living from Your love.*

Holy Spirit, what lies have I believed that prevent me from fully experiencing the God of love?

LIE:

Once you've written down every lie He shares with you, pray this prayer: *I renounce and break agreement with the lie that...*

Fill in the blank with the lies that He has revealed to you. Continue this prayer for each lie.

Holy Spirit, what's the truth?

TRUTH:

List the truth He shows you.

Or are you more like Chaya? Do you have a "hey look at me, I am here. Talk to me. Pay attention to me. Don't forget me. Don't leave me out" personality? Could this be rooted in performance, striving, or fear of being left out? I have to do, do, do for Father to notice me. I have to perform for love. I won't be outdone. Or is this just your larger than life, thriving, vibrant nature filling a room?

In the absence of relationship the only way to be known is through performance. The thing about performance is the fruit all looks the same. On the outside, it's charitable. It's kind. It's giving. It's loving. It's all the Godly traits it should be. However, if the motive of your heart behind your doing is rooted in fear and not love, it's performance based. If I have to make everything perfect because I'm concerned about what people will think, that's performance oriented. Performance is the hallmark of an orphan lifestyle. Jesus always commandeered a crowd wherever He went. Knowing who you are and what you carry is the hallmark of sonship. Sonship is attractive.

Let's ask Holy Spirit: *Holy Spirit, what is motivating my doing?*

If the answer was anything other than love, I invite you to pray this prayer with me: *I renounce and break agreement with performance. Jesus, I hand You performance, striving and fear of man. What would You like to give me in exchange for the need to perform for love?*

Be sure to record what He gives you.

I renounce and break agreement with the lie that I need to perform in order to receive God's acceptance or approval. I renounce and break agreement with the lie that the only way to be seen or known is to perform. Holy Spirit, what other lies have I believed about performance, striving and fear of man?

Holy Spirit, what's the truth?

Father, I repent for exalting the opinion of man above Your opinion of me. I repent for competing with others and needing to be seen. Father, what does it look like to live with Your stamp of approval on my life?

What does the God kind of life look like for me?

Father God, who am I and what do I carry?

Are you like Jeremiah? God so wants to bless you, He wants to give you good things, but you have not because you ask not. You are not really sure that God is in a good mood. You are not really sure that He loves you. You are not really sure that you can trust Him. You're not really sure that it is okay to come up and give Him a hug or give Him a kiss.

But the Father is saying to you, "My child, all that I have is yours. It's all yours. You were mine from the beginning. Even while you were yet in sin, I loved you. I have always loved you. I have never not loved you. Even now, I am pouring My love into you. Trust Me without question. Let Me provide for you. I'm really good at it."

If you can identify with Jeremiah, it's time for some real talk between you and Papa God. I invite you to use your own words, but I'll pen a few in case you need some help getting started. Be sure to pause and listen after you ask each question: *God, I'm not really sure about You. I know people say You are good and You're in a good mood. But I don't know that I've experienced Your goodness in my life. To be truthful, I'm not really sure that I can trust You. It's been so many times that I've needed things and You haven't come through for me. I'm angry about it. I no longer want to ask You for anything because I can't bear being disappointed yet again. I realize that I've built a case against You and that's exactly what the devil wanted me to do. I'm sorry for that. God would You come and take all of this hurt, all of the doubt, the mistrust, the suspicion away so that I can see You for who You really are? God, who do You want to be to me? Can I really trust You? Can I really experience You loving me?*

Holy Spirit, what lies have I believed that's caused me to doubt the goodness of God? Holy Spirit, what's Your truth? Father God, where have You been good in my life?

Holy Spirit, what lies have I believed that's caused me to mistrust God? Holy Spirit, what's the truth? Father God, where have You met my needs?

Holy Spirit, what lies have I believed that's caused me to be angry with God? Holy Spirit, what's the truth? Father God, what do You want my heart to believe about You?

Holy Spirit, what lies have I believed that's caused me to be disappointed in my relationship with God? Holy Spirit, what's the truth? Father God, how do You want me to see You?

Father God, I repent. I see now that I have seen You wrongly and I've judged You to be something You're not. I renounce and break agreement with every lie that has influenced me to have a wrong perspective of who You are. Drain those lies out of me and everything that came with them. Holy Spirit, thank You for the truth. I receive Your truth into every part of me.

Perhaps none of my children are an adequate representation of who you are and how you relate to Father God. Let me encourage you to take a moment with Holy Spirit to think about your relationship with Father God. What do you believe to be true about Him? How do you receive love from Him? How do you respond to His love? How do you give love to Father God?

Take a moment to record this exchange in your journal.

Think about it, what would it be like to totally rely on Father God? Father is the source of all things. He allows people, employment, opportunities, and things to be resources for His kids. But every good and perfect gift comes from the Father above in whom there is no shifting or variation.[33]

Perhaps you have been wrestling in your own strength to be provision, to make provision, to figure it all out. Today Father wants you to trust Him, to come to a place of rest. Freedom from anxiety and worry is available for you. Provision is His job, not yours.

---

33 James 1:17

For others, you have been relying on yourself, your spouse, your parents, your friends, but not on God. Father wants to give you a grace today to be able to fully rely on Him.

Holy Spirit, what does living interdependent and reliant upon Father God look like?

Be sure to record what He shows you.

CHAPTER 21

FINDING FATHER

God is love.[34] He manifests Himself as Healer, Provider, Protector, Friend, Goodness, Comforter, Redeemer, Teacher, Nurturer, Companion, Warrior, Judge, etc. In the Old Testament, no one really knew God in an intimate and personal manner and thus used the things He did to describe who He is. Then Jesus shows up on the scene and He says to the Scribes and Pharisees no one knows the Father except the Son.[35] And other than the moment on the cross when Jesus became our sin,[36] this Son who knows the Father so well only refers to Him by one name... Father. Although He manifests His character and nature in several different ways, He desires to be known by one simple, love filled name and that is Father.

When we commune with Him, He sows the seed of His nature into our hearts.[37] When He deposits His sperma (Greek word for seed) in us, we reproduce the fruit of His Spirit. The fruit of the Spirit is love.[38] The fruit of the Spirit is as multifaceted as the nature of God. Love manifests itself as joy, peace, patience, kindness, goodness, meekness and self-control.[39]

---

34   1 John 4:8
35   Matthew 11:27
36   Matthew 27:46
37   1 John 3:9
38   Galatians 5:22
39   Galatians 5:22-23

The absence of experiential love causes us to strive or toil. We were not designed for striving. We don't strive to produce fruit. We don't even have to strive to be righteous.[40] We don't have to strive to be something that we already are. The blood of Jesus makes us righteous. Fruitfulness flows from intimacy.

How does the seed from an apple become an apple tree? Or an acorn a mighty oak? Just as the fruit is in the seed, so the fruit of love abides in our hearts because we are made in His image and likeness. We have His seed. God is our real Father and we come from Him. Our embracing a resurrected lifestyle and walking out our union with Jesus causes this seed of love to blossom and flourish, in my opinion.

A tree spreads its branches outward and upward soaking in sunrays, allowing the heavens to water it and receives nutrients from the soil. As its roots grow deep, the tree matures and becomes all that it was intended to be.

John 15:5 *"I am the vine, you are the branches; he who abides in Me and I in him, he bears much fruit, for apart from Me you can do nothing."*

This is the act of grace for the New Testament believer. Grace is the operational power of God to do what we can't do on our own. No amount of striving, work or toil will produce the fruit of the Spirit in your life. No amount of striving to be holy will produce holiness in your life. Simply turn aside like the tree, extend your hands and your heart outward and upward in worship and allow the Son to shine on you. Receive the nutrients of the living Word of God and allow the Presence of Holy Sprit to rain upon you. As you abide, the seed of life, the seed of love will begin to germinate and mature.

When Jesus cried out, "It is finished,"[41] He meant it. There remains for you a Sabbath rest.[42] Learn to do the hard work of rest. You no longer are required to do to be. Because God is, I AM that I AM,[43] we can be

---

40   Romans 5:19
41   John 19:30
42   Hebrews 4:9
43   Exodus 3:14

all that He has destined us to be. Righteousness is lived out in our being, not our doing.

There is no law that can prevail over the law of love.[44] Why? Because where the Spirit of the Lord is there is freedom.[45] It's been said that increased levels of His presence equals increased levels of freedom. For the New Covenant believer, our reality is fullness.[46] We already have ALL of God,[47] so we can be completely FREE! This is GOOD NEWS! Is greatness crying out from within you? Maintain a lifestyle of abiding and communing, do the hard work of rest. Soak in the Son and then go out and live in freedom.[48]

Listen with your spirit to *Ephesians 1:7(MSG)"Because of the sacrifice of the Messiah, his blood poured out on the altar of the Cross, we're a free people---free of penalties and punishments chalked up by all our misdeeds. And not just barely free, either. Abundantly free!"*

What would it be like to be free? Truly free. What does freedom look like to the believer? How do you handle God's freedom? How do you live in freedom? Love in freedom? Show honor in freedom?

Love allows you to rightly handle your freedom and manage your options well. When we live from love and govern our lives according to Father's love for us, everything in us will make protecting the love that flows between God and us a priority.

Relationships are the most important thing to Father God. He's far more concerned about you connecting with Him and connecting with others than He is about what you can do for Him. Father has such a deep profound love for you. Learn to live in His love. Learn to live from His love.

When faced with despair, do we instinctively react with emotions of

---

44   Galatians 5:23
45   2 Corinthians 3:17
46   Ephesians 1:23
47   Colossians 2:9
48   Acts 17:28

discouragement and disillusionment or do we choose to command our bodies to take a deep breath and think on the Lord and His goodness? When faced with crisis, do we instinctively panic or do we command our bodies to remain calm and think with our renewed minds for Holy Spirit inspired wisdom?

In my human wisdom, this sounded so noble until James Jordan, director of Fatherheart Ministries[49] in Taupo, New Zealand helped me realize that me controlling my reaction was still me directing my mind, will and emotions. And just like I can direct my mind, will and emotions to behave one way. I can wake up tomorrow and direct them to behave in the complete opposite manner. John wrote in 3 John 1:2 that it was his prayer for us be in health and prosper even as our soul prospers. A prosperous soul is the result of a human spirit being divinely and intimately connected to Holy Spirit. This alone leads to optimum levels of freedom.

I have noticed that all too often many believers seem to ride a roller coaster of emotional healing. One month, they are good, stable and have it all together. The next month, they are navel gazing, jacked up and in deep despair. Often baffled by the inconsistencies in the emotional state of these who bear the image and likeness of Christ, I began to ask Holy Spirit to show me the key for constancy.

Jesus says He is the same yesterday today and forever.[50] And 1 John 4:17 says, *"as He is so are we in this world."* So if Jesus can be constant throughout time and I have the mind of Christ,[51] it seems only right that I should be able to live constant in my walk with the Godhead despite situations or circumstance. It was in this quest for an answer that Father began to teach me the greater grace of living from a transformed heart.

Another truth I learned from James is that even if I get my act together and control my response, if my heart isn't healed, it's still just that…an act. Living a transformed life is not learning how to act and then by

---

49   www.fatherheart.net
50   Hebrews 13:8
51   1 Corinthians 2:16

sheer human determination doing it. Sheer human determination is us simply directing our will or our mind to rule. God doesn't pour His love into our mind, will or our feelings. He pours His love into our hearts.[52] As the Holy Spirit connects with our spirit, our spirit man becomes prominent. Our spirit is designed to lead our soul and our body. For all who are being led by the Spirit of God, these are the sons of God.[53]

When Father's love is poured into our hearts, we are different. Every part of us becomes healed, becomes whole. Every encounter with Truth is an encounter with Love. For God is love. And the experience of Father loving us causes us to see things differently. His love fills me, heals me, and transforms me.

When my heart is transformed, I will automatically do differently. I won't have to think about it. I won't need to command my body or direct my will to behave in a righteous manner. I will automatically respond through love as my heart is transformed into the righteousness of God in Christ Jesus. Because the righteousness of God in Christ is who I am and your heart is who you are. All the issues of life flow from the place of who we are. This is why we are encouraged in Proverbs to guard our heart with fidelity, to keep watch over it with truth.

When I am hurt, I am able to run to Him and have a truthful exchange. Handing Him my hurt and taking in His love, He heals me. Love allows me to see people differently. Love allows me to believe the best about people even when past experience says differently.

The goal in life is not to become healed. The goal in life is to become loved. Everything that God is is found in His great love for us. Everything that we are to become, we become as His love transforms us. His love allows us to be who we already are. His love grants us full permission to be one with His Son, Jesus, while living out the reality of that union every day.[54]

---

52   Romans 5:5
53   Romans 8:14
54   Colossians 3:4

Father's love isn't just an attitude towards us. It isn't just something we know in our head. His love is a continual experience that is constantly being poured into our hearts by the Holy Spirit. Many of us don't realize that our lives actually begin at the cross. Jesus bought our past. It no longer belongs to us. We've been cut off from our past. But because this truth hasn't been revealed to us, the enemy continues to use the hurts, lies, wounds and pains of our past to torment us and wreak havoc in our lives. The pain of these offenses seemingly speak louder than the truth of who we are today as a resurrected person. So we come into agreement with pain, offense and lies forming blocks that prevent us as new creations in Christ from fully embracing and receiving the continual experience of Father loving us. What we fail to realize is that every wall we've erected to keep pain and hurt at bay also prevents us from experiencing Father loving us.

Every wound in our life has come because we've experienced something other than love. Those wounds create fear; create walls. They cause us to shrink back, cause us to lash out. Only the Father's amazingly perfect agape love casts out fear. Only the love of God can heal you and make your heart whole. Love is the fulfillment of every need in our life.

The truth is, the very nature of God has been poured into us by the Holy Spirit to completely change us and make us different, make us new, make us just like Him. The Father aims the love in His heart at liberating His sons and daughters. There's been much teaching recently on identity throughout Christendom and that's wonderful. However, identity without nurture leaves us incomplete. Yes, the Father gives us our identity but it is the Mothering Love of Father God that repairs the breech of the unhealed places. It is the Motherheart of God that comforts and nurtures and propels us into a place of security and confidence that frees us from striving, competition, comparison and ambition. It is the very Mothering Love of Father God that says, "I am enough. I am loved. I am wanted. He sees me."

Ephesians 1:3 in the Message Translation says it best, *"Long before he laid down earth's foundations, he had us in mind, had settled on us as the focus of his love, to be made whole and holy by his love."*

He whom the Son sets free is free indeed. You are free to be whole. You are free to be holy. Freedom is simply you learning to live loved. What does you living loved look like?

What would life look like for you being fully and completely loved by Perfect Love? Because you are! Revelation is simply the unveiling of truth that has been there all along. And the truth is that Jesus in a most extreme and furious act of love by dying on the cross for you removed every block, hindrance and obstacle that would prevent you from experiencing His Father loving you. From the moment Jesus cried out, "It is finished," separation has never again been an issue for us. Truthfully, the lamb was slain before the foundation of the world was laid which means, separation has NEVER been an issue for God. On our end, we need to believe that there is no longer anything between Father and us and just simply receive His love.

I don't make light of this process. I know some people say they have tried and tried to feel Father loving them and they just can't. What I have come to know is that we reproduce our idea of normal. So if we think it's normal not to experience God loving us, then we won't experience it. What we believe to be true is absolutely true to us.

Sometimes the sheer incapacity to receive Father's love is tied to what we believe to be true about love. In some ways, I think I was like that. My momma's love hurt. It was marked with beatings, cruel punishments, harsh words, and scornful looks. My father's love hurt. It was marked with invisibility, indifference, absence, and emotional distancing. My boyfriend's love hurt. It was marked by misuse, rejection, betrayal and abandonment.

If love as we've experienced it looks like lies, control, abuse, anger, rage, violence, rejection, abandonment, what in the world would love from Almighty God who created the universe look like?

In my home, growing up, parental love looked like obligation. I had the necessities: food, water, clothing, and shelter. I had correction.

My mom didn't have any problem with beating my behind when I did wrong. I had very little touch that wasn't punishment. I had very little communication that wasn't criticism. I had very little eye contact unless it was to give me "the eye." You know the one? The if you don't straighten up, I'm gonna beat your behind eye.

Without an accurate experience of Father loving us and a true revealing of God as Father, pastors, teachers, evangelists all over the world have re-presented their image of parental love onto Father God. Their portrayal of Father God along with our own personal experiences of parental love may cause us to waver in our belief that Father could really truly love us.

Yet, I believe there is something innate in all of us that knows Father is suppose to be loving and kind, so we end up with a duplicit message that resembles a good cop/bad cop interrogation scene. For most of us, we blindly accept the message, thinking this is just how God is. Staying on the ever-present roller coaster of our emotions, having good days and bad days never giving voice to what our hearts are really feeling because we don't want to rock the boat and upset the bad cop.

But, if we were to be honest with ourselves, how could we ever trust someone who isn't really for us? How could we ever be devoted to someone who doesn't have our best interest at heart?

So what does satan do? He continues to misrepresent Father God to us and get us to come into agreement with lies about Him.

His lying voice whispers to our soul: *He's not for me. I can't trust Him. He never comes through. God could never love me. He let me lose my house. He gave me this cancer. He allowed my baby to die. Could He really love me? Could He really want me? Why in the world would God be interested in me? Does He just want to use me? Make me a servant?*

I couldn't fathom how God, Almighty God could possibly love me, knowing all that I had done; all the bad choices I made. I couldn't bring myself to look up. I couldn't imagine myself worthy enough, good enough, clean enough to gain His approval. I was blind but now I see.

Then one day Truth opened up the passage of the prodigal son in Luke 15 to help me see the power of Love. In Luke 15:20, the father runs to meet the son to provide a passage of safety through the valley of death. I've heard it said that he did this to protect the son from the stoning he deserved for disgracing the father. By running, the father would bring shame upon himself as distinguished men of the Jewish culture wore a robe like garment and to run, the father would have had to lift the outer garment of his clothing and expose his linen undergarment to freely move his legs. So very simply, the men did not run. Yet, here is this father running to meet his son. Love covers.

In verses 21-22 of the same passage, the father covers the sins of his son with his blessing and favor by giving the son a robe, a ring and sandals for his feet. Interrupting the son's sob story, love covers. Many ministers have preached that repentance was the son saying to his father I have sinned. Repentance actually happened the moment the son changed his mind for the better and remembered the love and generosity of his dad. For it was at that moment that the son believed in his heart and sat out to return home.

It's the lovingkindness of God that leads to repentance, not His punishment or His disapproval.

Why would we ever want to hang around someone who disapproves of us? But someone who loves me. Someone who is for me. Someone who will remind me of my worth, my value. Everything in me wants to go home and be with that Father. Love covers.

There is Jesus on the cross. Him who knew no sin becoming sin for us so that we could know His Dad.[55] Every sin from Adam to the last person to be born before a new heaven and a new earth[56] emerges was heaped upon Him. Why? Love covers.

This type of love produces a trust that makes me absolutely secure in who I am and who He is for me. How can I trust God steadily?

---

55   2 Corinthians 5:21; John 14:6
56   Revelation 21:1

Because "as He is, so are we in this world." Jesus modeled the greatest act of trust as He lay dying on the cross. Even in the most tortuous act of crucifixion, as He breathed His last breath, Jesus cried out, "Father into your hands I commit my spirit."[57] Father, I trust Your love for me. I trust Your goodness towards me. Father, I surrender my spirit to you.

Without submission there can be no lasting commitment. Wm. Paul Young wrote in his book, *The Shack*, "Submission is not control. It's true surrendering." There on the cross, Jesus was saying to His Father, I can surrender My heart, my will, even My life to You because I believe in Your great love for me. I know You are committed to loving Me well.

How could Jesus say that? Because He knew His dad. He knew firsthand that He was good. That He is love. That He is light. That He is life.

This is the Father we need to become acquainted with. The One who loves us. The one who isn't disillusioned or disappointed by us. The Father who is there.

This man (Jesus) walked through hell for me that I could know His Dad. Not the misrepresentation of His Father but His Dad, the good Father; the perfect Father.

I don't remember one time growing up hearing a preacher say the Father loves you. I remember a lot of rules and being told what I couldn't do. I was told about all of the bad things God would do to me if I broke the rules. But I remember nothing at all about love. Nothing.

We sang Jesus loves me. So I knew in my head that Jesus loved me. I knew that He died for me. But knowing that I'm loved and being loved, feeling loved are two completely different things.

Back to the duplicity of the good cop/bad cop message, Jesus was good. Father God was bad, or at the very least, mean. Jesus is your friend. Father God is your punisher. But that's not true. God's not

---

57   Luke 23:46

schizophrenic. He is the same yesterday, today and forever.

The same. The Father Himself loves you. Jesus loves you because He first saw the Father loving you. Jesus loves you because He and His Father are one. In fact, Father is loving you right now.

Father God is the one who teaches, counsels, reproves us, loves us, and cheers us on. He violently tore the heavens to reach His kids. "This is my beloved Son in whom I am well pleased. This is my Son, hear him." This is the Motherheart of God reaching through the heavens loving with His comforting love.

And Jesus saying to the masses, This is my Father and your Father. This is who He is.

Ex. 3:14 (MSG) God said to Moses, "I-AM-WHO-I-AM. Tell the People of Israel, 'I-AM sent me to you.'"

I am Healer. I am Provider. I am Comforter. I am Protector. I am Present. I am Truth. I am Love. I Light. I am Life. I am Friend. I am Peace. I am Joy. I am Goodness. I am the One who sees, the God who hears.

While every one of these statements about God is accurate, Jesus summed up His name best. He called Him: Father. Everything you ever wanted to experience in the Personhood of God is found inside of His fathering relationship to you.

2 Cor. 6:18 "And I will be a Father to you and you shall be My sons and daughters, says the Lord Almighty. "

When I really see Father for who He is, as He is; I will begin to paint the earth with the nature of God. This is why the earth was created, to fill the earth and subdue it. Fill it with what? The glory of the Father. The earth was created for you to display ALL of Father God throughout the planet. Because as He is, so are we in this world.

The ultimate revelation Jesus brought to us was of His Father.

Hebrews 1:3 says, "He is the exact representation of the Father." Bill Johnson always says Jesus Christ is perfect theology. Anything you want to know about Father God you can find in the person of Jesus. Completely blows a hole in the good cop/bad cop myth.

Trust and hope is swallowed up in love. It's easy for me to trust steadily when I believe that I am loved. I can't help but be confident in the One who is for me, the One who has my back.

It's a simple thing to hope unswervingly when I have received Father's extravagant love in my heart. No amount of circumstance can uproot my confident expectation that good is coming to me when I know that I am loved by my Heavenly Father.

Where love abounds there is plenty of hope and joy. *When dreams come true there is hope and joy. Desire realized is a tree of life.*[58]

Look at the word desire. De is a prefix that means out of and sire means father or male parent. Could it be possible that the desire within us is born out of Father?

He is for you. He is never not for you. He wants to see your dreams come true even more than you do. What matters to you, matters to Him. He longs to partner with you.

Once God sets His love upon us, He never lets up. He aims His love at anything that stands between us being able to receive and contain even more of His love. He aims His love at every lie we've believed. And through the Holy Spirit, He begins to bring truth. He aims His love at every wound, every pain, and every place of trauma. He arrives into those soul/spirit hurts, with healing in His wings, bringing a fresh perspective which is the mind of Christ; removing the reproach. There's no scorn or mockery in His eyes. He is wholly, madly, and passionately in love with you. The look of love so genuine, so real, so deep it will completely and woefully ravish your heart.

---

58   Proverbs 13:12

There is nothing you can do to earn Father's love. You can't pray enough, fast enough, give more money to gain His acceptance or His approval. When Father looks at you, His heart swells with love for you.

And likewise, there is nothing you can do to make Father love you less. You can't sin more, give less, steal more, go to church less, backslide more. He is fervent in His love for you and that love remains constant forever. In fact, the Word tells us, that *while we were yet sinners, Christ died for us.* [59]

The King has brought you to His banqueting table. His banner over you is love. His deepest desire is to hear you laugh and to see you free. He desires for you to live completely secure and steadfast in His love for you.

I believe that Father so delights in you, in me, in all of us. I believe that it is His good pleasure to give us the Kingdom. I believe that the Father Himself loves me, loves you. I believe, in fact, that even as you read this, the Father is loving you right now. Even as you inhale, He is pouring His love into Your heart.

Father loving us is more than a feeling. Just as we receive salvation by faith, we receive the experience of Father loving us by faith. *We believe in our hearts that God has been raised from the dead and we are saved.* [60] We believe in our hearts that Father is loving us right now and we are loved. *Proverbs 23:7 says, "For as he thinks within himself, so he is."* If I think I am loved, then I am. Conversely, if you don't know with your heart that you are loved, freedom has no place to flow freely in your life. What is your heart telling you?

We cannot love effectively if we have not been loved extravagantly. Father God is the wellspring of Love. He is awakening His kids to living fully loved by Him, having the mind of Christ, and cultivating a friendship with Holy Spirit. There is a higher place for us to live from and that place is the Father's heart.

---

59   Romans 5:8
60   Romans 10:9

Father God longs for the day when we are so secure in His love for us - who He is to us and who we are in Him - that the cares of life no longer rock us or cause us to be unsettled. When we know who our Daddy is, we can hear His affirmations, whether loudly spoken or softly whispered. We hear Him. He wants us to move from living in a place where our confidence and total reliance on Him is pockmarked with fear and doubt. Father longs to completely love the fear and doubt away. Perfect love casts out fear.

When Father God fully loves you and you see Him as He is, you will begin to rest in His protection and provision. When you behold Him, you can easily identify things that are incongruent with His character. When you experience the love of God, it makes you confident. Love destroys all fear.

Father God once said to me, "Every part of your mind that is not supernaturally transformed will be at war with My goodness. There is so much good in My heart for you. Only the renewed mind can completely receive all that I hold in My heart for you." Father's love transforms.

When I experience the love of God, I stop being afraid. I live fearless. I live boldly. I live confidently. I live with honest expectancy of God's goodness in my life. Father wants us to live with openness of heart.

This revelation of Father's love is to be the foundation upon which we build our lives. It is from this place that we live and move and have our being.[61] Only in the love of God do we truly find life.

Love begins with He first loved me. And because of His great love, I love Him. I love me. Out of the great love affair of Him loving me and me receiving His love, I learn to freely give His love away.

Father is pursuing His kids to simply love us, to cherish us, to hold us, to redeem us because we are His own. He is longing for the communion of His sons and daughters. He is longing to see His kids live love out loud.

---

61   Acts 17:28

CHAPTER 22

FINDING ME

Many of the people who know the Felicia I am today have no idea who I used to be. And the truth is, that Felicia is dead. She died when Jesus died.[62] But because no one told me she was dead, I treated my new me in Christ - the resurrected me - as if she was the old Adamic Felicia. Colossians 3:9-10 (MSG) speaks the truth for everyone who is born again, *"You're done with that old life. Every item of your new way of life is custom made by the Creator, with His label on it."*

Instead of living from the tree of life, I was still responding to life through the tree of the knowledge of good and evil. So Father in His loving kindness, allowed me to encounter Truth and in those encounters His love completely washed me clean.

On August 23, 2009, I had a vivid encounter with Truth. As a birthday gift to myself, I filled our Jacuzzi tub with lavender bath salts and settled in for a nice long soak. I'd set my cd player on repeat with Kimberly & Alberto Rivera playing in the background. I laid my head back on the bath pillow and closed my eyes. As I did, I began to hear so clearly the voice of Love speaking to me. And this is what He said, "I have loved you with an everlasting love. The day I formed you, knitted you,

---

62 Romans 6:8; Colossians 2:20; Colossians 3:3

fashioned you, my eyes were upon you - glued to you. My precious one, I created you with strength. I put ore in you and blew on the embers with the wind of my fire. I fashioned you, knitted you, handcrafted you. I poured faith in you. I gave you leadership and strength; broad shoulders to carry the weight of my anointing. I gifted you with song and poured a well of worship deep, deep, deep into you, an effervescent pool of love bubbling up from within. I gave you wisdom, insight, discerning of spirits. "What else," I cried, "what else can I give to this one I love so dearly? What can I give to this champion, this warrior woman of mine?" Strength, Courage, Boldness, Understanding, Revelation, Grace, Grace, and more Grace. Ah Yes!! I shall give her My favor to go with her, to open doors, to prepare the way...and resiliency. Yes, Spirit, she shall need resiliency and endurance for the long haul. Wow, Father! Look at her! Look at what You've created. Isn't she beautiful? You should call her joy, happy. Yes, Son, I shall put it in the heart of her family to call her Felicia. For a season, she shall walk and her identity will be veiled. She will be called out of her name and will not know or recognize all that is within her but then a day shall come, surely even now the hour is upon her, where she shall arise and declare herself blessed of the Lord. So much beauty in her name. Yes, indeed Father, beautiful."

I was overcome with gratitude that Love Himself would allow me to hear the song He sang over me as He knit me and placed me in my mother's womb. I dried my hands as quickly as possible and grabbed my journal, which lay cast aside on my vanity nearby. I wanted to pen the Love encounter lest I forget one word that was spoken.

"Felicia," Father said to me, "I have such a profound love for you. When you have a revelation of My love, you'll learn to live in My love, live from My love and fashion and govern your life according to My love for you."

Through my encounters with Truth, I've found a love that's greater than life itself. When I look into His eyes, I see acceptance. I see passion. I see love. I see me, the way He sees me. I am becoming what I am beholding.

I have been given an assignment of love. Father has commissioned me to share my life and how He's loved me. He wooed me. He pursued me.

His love washes over me. His love envelops me. His love surrounds me. His love frees me. His love draws me in. His love empowers me, believes in me, celebrates me. His love draws me upward into a greater sense of who I am in Him. The greatest gift I can give the world is to love as He does.

Love is enough because God is enough. Love compels me to live Jesus. Love compels me to agree with the blueprint of who Father created me to be before He ever placed me in my mother's womb. I cannot live in love without thinking differently about God and myself.

Why is it important that we know Father God loves us? Knowing that you are loved gives you a sense of belonging. You know who you are. It is the root of your identity. Knowing you are loved gives you safety and protection. Knowing you are loved fills you with security. You have a home. You are covered. You are provided for. You are not alone. Bill Johnson says, "You + God = A Majority." God is for you.

A few years ago, Father said to me, "There are annals and annals of documents in my heart of how to release love on the earth." I asked, "Father, how do I access those annals?" He replied, "You have the key to unlock the secrets that are inside My heart. There are many depths inside My heart. Every living thing, every created thing lives inside My heart. Life flows from My heart."

The mission of love is the restoration of sons and daughters to the Father. Love is the structure in which freedom is governed. True love from the Godhead sets a new standard. Love expressed is living from the tree of life. It is living in relationship with Father, Jesus and Holy Spirit. You are part of the family of God.

There has to be a revelation of the Father before there can be a relationship as a son. If you never have a revelation of God as Father, you'll always live as a servant in the Master's house only knowing him as Lord. The truth is God doesn't want to use you. You're not some tool to be used and discarded when you get blunt or are no longer fit for use. He wants to participate with you in life. He's not interested in having more servants. He wants you to join Him as a partner in the family business.

What is the mission of the family business? Love. What is the vision for the family business? Love. What are the goals and objective of the family business? Love. What is the trademark of our family business? Love. What are we, as a family, known for? Love.

Love is who He is. He can never not love you. This is the intimacy that comes from abiding in the vine. Intimacy, Danny Silk breaks the word down as, into me you see.

Look into me. See the depth of my love for You. See how my heart beats for You. This is my Father and your Father. This is His great love for you. Radical, extreme, extravagant - furious is His love for you.

Listen with your spirit to 1 Corinthians 13:10,13(MSG), *We know only a portion of the truth, and what we say about God is always incomplete. But when the Complete arrives, our incompletes will be canceled...But for right now, until that completeness, we have three things to do to lead us toward that consummation: Trust steadily in God, hope unswervingly, love extravagantly. And the best of the three is love.*

This is why Father God could send Jesus because He knew Jesus loved Him like this. That He trusted steadily in God, hoped unswervingly, loved Him extravagantly.

He knew that Jesus was 100% secure in His identity as a son and that He would not cave under pressure.

John 13:34-35 says, *"A new commandment I give to you, that you love one another, even as I have loved you, that you also love one another. By this all men will know that you are My disciples, if you have love for one another."*

If the world will know that we are His disciples by our love, perhaps we've missed the fullness of our calling. What if the great commission was really to live the great commandment? What if instead of teaching people what we thought, we taught them how to love? What would it look like to fully love God, love yourself, love others?

God has called us to be love, to live loved and to give His love away. In so doing, we introduce others to the lovingkindness of God that leads to repentance. When we live the great commandment, we will fulfill the great commission.

I bless you to encounter Truth and to become what you behold. May you come to intimately know the One who is the giver and sustainer of all life. Gazing into the water, may you see laughter in His face and eyes full of love for you. Pausing by the water's reflection, my soul remembers who I am (Psalm 23, Mirror Translation). Mirroring the truth that indeed He created you and knows everything about you. Overwhelmed by the depth of this unconditional love, may you lean back on the plush grass and look up. Even there, may you see, His banner over you is love.[63]

---

63 Song of Songs 2:4

THE TRIUNE GOD

Why don't you just say God? Why do you sometimes use Jesus, sometimes say Holy Spirit and sometimes say Father God?

I believe in the Trinitarian God, one God existing in three distinct powerful persons each having their own distinct individual personalities. There is only one God. Father (Abba, Papa, Daddy God) is God, Jesus is God, and Holy Spirit is God. The Father is not Jesus, Jesus is not the Father, and the Father is not Holy Spirit. In the nature of Father God, we derive our identity and we receive provision and protection. Jesus is our Big Brother, our Savior, our King and Lord. We know through scripture that Holy Spirit is our Comforter, Teacher, and Nurturer. He is the One who helps you grow and develop, our come alongside friend; the Spirit of Truth He is called.

Most often, the name I use when asking a question of God depends on the aspect of His nature that I need to draw upon at the time. You feel free to use the name that you are most comfortable with. Just as I have personally encountered Truth, I found that I have also encountered Father and Holy Spirit. Addressing the Godhead by their individual personalities helps me to know them in intimacy and power and not just form.

*Eph. 3:14-15 For this reason, I bow my knee to the **Father** from whom every family in heaven and on earth derives its name...*

*Eph. 1: 3-9(MSG) He's the **Father** of our Master, Jesus Christ...He thought of everything, provided for everything we could possibly need.*

Is. 27:5 Or let him rely on My protection, Let him make peace with

Me, Let him make peace with Me.

*Rom. 8:27 For those whom He foreknew, He also predestined to become conformed to the image of **His Son**, so that He would be the firstborn among many brethren*

1 Tim. 6:14-15 that you keep the commandment without stain or reproach until the appearing of our Lord Jesus Christ, which He will bring about at the proper time—He who is the blessed and only Sovereign, the King of kings and Lord of lords

*John 14:26 But the Comforter, [even] the **Holy Spirit**, whom the Father will send in my name, he shall teach you all things, and bring to your remembrance all that I said unto you.*

My Mom...

This is my disclaimer. As I have shared vulnerably and transparently with you, it may seem that I have judged my mom or dishonored her. Please know that that is not my heart or my intent in sharing. I wanted you, the reader, to hear the heart of the wounded girl at ages five, twelve, sixteen, etc. and to experience my mom through the lens that I perceived her through.

As Holy Spirit has healed my heart, He helps me every day to see my mom as Father God sees her. My mom is an amazing woman; a brilliant intercessor who loves the Lord with all of her heart and loves her family. She is incredibly generous in her time, her love and her finances.

One of the things God has shown me as He has healed many broken places in me is that life events are skewed through the perception of the participant. I'm sure if you were to ask my mom, my dad or my brother about the same events that I have chronicled here you would receive a different rendering from their perception. You've received the perception of a wounded child. I chose not to clean that up or pretty it up, not to paint my mom in a negative light but to help you see a vivid picture of the lies and ungodly beliefs Papa had to heal in me. Our perceptions power our emotional responses and fuel our paradigms. The healing journey for us all is to bring our perceptions and perspective in complete alignment with Truth.

Every day in my relationship with my mom, I now have a choice. I can choose to see her through those broken wounded painful hurtful places or I can choose to see her through the lens of love. I am in no ways perfect at loving. There are days that I struggle with "choosing to love as an act of my will" and loving from the heart as Father loves. But I have endeavored in my adult relationship with my mom to open my heart and to love her. This is a process, one that I walk through in great humility with Father, Jesus and Holy Spirit.

Which leads me to another important lesson I've learned through these Truth encounters, just because my relationship with Papa, Jesus and Holy Spirit has been restored doesn't automatically mean my familial relationships on earth have been restored. In truth, I'm holding out for restoration in many areas. But know this, a relationship requires the participation of at least two people who are 100% responsible for their part in the relationship. The beautiful thing about life in Abba is that nothing is impossible to Him.

To that end, you need to know that I have an amazing mom that I love. I'm thankful that she chose to give me life. And I am grateful for her heart of love towards me.

It should also be noted that this disclaimer covers my dad and my extended paternal family. My heart is not to uncover, but to help someone else in their God journey by being as completely transparent as I know to be. I love my family and I am grateful that I was born into the family God placed me in. My perspective, right or wrong, is my perspective. What Papa has been teaching me has He has healed me and cleansed those unloved places is that when I live from the tree of life, it no longer matters who is right or who is wrong. I am free to love. As I grow and mature, He is teaching me how to do just that. I pray He will do the same for you as well. May Papa bless you abundantly and may you experience Him loving you in every area of your life.

All His Best,

Felicia

ACKNOWLEDGEMENTS

To Doug...my knight in shining armor. I cherish you. Thank you for sweeping me off my feet and encouraging me every step of the way. You've been my partner in this grand adventure called life and it's never been a dull moment. I've never had someone believe in me so completely and so fully as I've found in you. You are a man who embodies, "even when you are at your worse, you are safe with me." You have loved me in all of my brokenness and you love me still in all of my wholeness. Thank you for accepting me enough to see inside and still look me full on in the face and love me. If the men our girls marry are even half as good as you, they'll do just fine. Thank you for not allowing anyone or anything to cheat us out of our fun. With everything I am, I love you.

To Brittany, Tre', Chaya & Jeremiah...Murrell Tribe. What can I say? At times I feel like I've probably gotten more wrong than I have right, but thank you for letting me try. You are all collectively and individually incredibly breathtaking, resilient, beautiful and amazing. How great is our God to redeem familial relationships by giving me you. It is an extreme honor and privilege to be your mom. I love you.

Sherri Lewis, thank you seems too small a phrase for every part you've played in this work getting from my head to my laptop and finally into print. Thank you for sitting down with me at Tuscan Brio Grille almost four years ago and helping me to outline this book. Your constant nagging, er uh, ENCOURAGEMENT, is a huge part of this finished work. Thank you for your assistance with previewing this work numerous times and pushing me forward. I love you.

Dr. Joyce Lewis, thank you for being the first reader of this manuscript and for your belief in me. Lanell Drummer, thank you for writing the book summary. Without your eloquent words, the back cover may very well have remained blank. I am grateful for your friendship on this journey.

Kathy Brusnighan, thank you for the use of your prophetic art for my book cover. I greatly appreciate your amazing ability to hear and see what Papa is doing and express it so vividly through your creativity. To enjoy more of Kathy's art, please check out her website at www.kathybrusnighan.com

Christina Files and Sarah Delaney – editor and graphic designer extraordinaire. You are both amazing. Thank you for your contribution to this work and helping me bring this to fruition.

Trisha Frost, thank you – not only for your endorsement but also for your generosity and your belief in me. Without your unending support, this book may not have reached the finish line as quickly as it did. For that, I am incredibly and eternally grateful. Father's abundant blessing to you and Shiloh Place Ministries.

Papa, Jesus and Holy Spirit...we got 'er done! Thank you for extending Your circle of love to invite me into the Great Dance. It's my great delight to be a part of the family business. I'm honored to be Your little girl. I love that I get to play and participate in what You're doing. May You be glorified through these words.